Final Judgment & the Goodness of God

How does a loving God punish evil?

Scott Rogers

Final Judgment & the Goodness of God

by Scott Rogers

© **2019 by** Scott Rogers
All rights reserved.

Edited by Adam Colwell's WriteWorks, LLC: Adam Colwell
Cover Design by Jaime Anaya
Typesetting by Katherine Lloyd
Published by Adam Colwell's WriteWorks through Kindle
Direct Publishing

Printed in the United States of America
Print ISBN: 978-1-7324474-8-6
eBook ISBN: 978-1-7324474-9-3

Table of Contents

Acknowledgments & Dedication

This is my first published book, and in the process I discovered that writing a book is a much larger undertaking than I originally envisioned. It involves the contributions of many, and there are numerous people that I should acknowledge who assisted in bringing this vision to a completed work.

First is my wife, Nancy, who spent hours with me discussing these topics and encouraging me to communicate the ideas to a broader audience. I also want to thank others who provided input and feedback as the book was developing: John Childs, one of my past co-laborers in our development work in Mexico; John O'Hair, Bible teacher and past missionary; Jon Heine, missionary to international students; Pastor Shannon Huetter; and John McFadyen, my long-term friend with whom I have shared life on many different levels through the years. None of these would necessarily agree with every statement in this book, but their input was essential.

As I am not a Hebrew or Greek scholar, I have relied on the commentary of those scholars and theologians that I respect for the meanings of Hebrew and Greek words and their proper application. These scholars and their works are referenced in the back of this book, and it is very proper to acknowledge them. I also want to thank the individuals that reviewed and edited the numerous drafts: my wife, Nancy, my daughter, Heather Talag, and, of course, my primary editor, Adam Colwell, who provided the expertise to take a rough product and turn it into a readable book. Adam, along with his colleagues at Adam Colwell's WriteWorks, also provided invaluable knowledge and expertise in the design and formatting of the final book for publishing.

With any book about God and the kingdom of God, the Lord himself provides the vision and inspiration, given that the author is yielded to his leading. Without his Spirit, there is no true knowledge or discovery of spiritual truth. Ideally, the author is just the conduit through which God can communicate his eternal perspectives. No one who is seeking God wants to spend their valuable time reading what are merely the thoughts and ideas of a fallible human being, and so I have endeavored to allow God to express himself through my writing. Through his grace and mercy, God has given humans the incredible privilege of participating in his work of calling dead people to life through the proclamation of the gospel.

This book is dedicated to God, who shines light into darkness, to those living in the shadow of death.

A Quest for Answers

Every year, thousands of international students converge on the campuses of universities all over the country. Di Ya was one of them.

A Chinese architecture student at the University of Arizona, she was curious about the Christian faith. She sat in on many of the Bible studies I led at the campus ministry for international students, watched evangelistic films about the life of Christ, and heard many times about God's love demonstrated to us through Christ—but she remained somewhat skeptical.

As usual, we were meeting at a residence near the university, and the students were gathering before the start of the study. She came up to me and asked, point blank, "So if I don't believe in Jesus, then I will go to hell?"

I'd heard that someone had told Di Ya that according to the Bible hell was a place of unending punishment and everyone who is not a Christian goes there to be tormented by God forever. "Well, God is a just and fair God," I said, "and he punishes people only when necessary, and only those who really deserve it."

I instantly knew my response was inadequate, and it was clear Di Ya was not persuaded by my weak answer. It was one of the last meetings she attended. She eventually left the fellowship without coming to faith in Christ.

A Christian for over 45 years, I have led Bible studies to countless groups and individuals for most of those years. I have served God a number of years in Latin America, discipling and helping to plant churches in various remote areas.

Through my involvement in international student ministry, I have discussed the gospel with students from all over the world: China, India, Malaysia, Singapore, Vietnam, Egypt, and several Latin American countries.

But after the encounter with Di Ya, I realized that I was really not qualified to represent the Lord on the subject of the final judgment. I had a firm understanding of salvation through faith in Christ, and of God's justice and judgment in a general sense. But I had never really thought through or searched the Scripture to gain a full understanding of what the Bible says specifically about the final judgment and punishment.

Needless to say, I was disappointed in myself that I was not able to give a clear and definitive answer to Di Ya's most important question. Her query, or a version of it, had been asked by others, and each time I responded with ambiguity. I determined to resolve that problem by discovering what the Bible actually said about this vital topic.

I poured over Scripture for the next several years and conducted in-depth studies on all the terms and passages related to the final judgment and punishment in the Bible. I eventually came to some definite conclusions. The results were surprising and not at all what I expected to find because they were different from what I heard previously from some pastors and radio preachers. In the process of my study on the final judgment, I came upon a myriad of scriptures that speak to the issue of how God judges *all* people, including those who have never heard the gospel message of salvation through faith in Christ.

Today, I believe I can now confidently answer Di Ya's question and others like it. Sadly, I saw Di Ya a couple more times during my time of study, but she was no longer interested so the subject was not brought up again. It is my prayer that God will send someone else to her to finish a task I left undone.

So what is the nature of the final judgment? When will it occur? On what basis will humans be judged? What will be the final end of the wicked? What will be the nature of their punishment? How will God finally culminate his plan for all people? These are the questions *Final Judgment & the Goodness of God* will address—and I hope that you will be persuaded by what I discovered.

Most Christians have basic assumptions and beliefs about God's final judgment and end-time punishment. However, similar to my experience with Di Ya, many can't articulate or defend their beliefs on these subjects. This is because they have not thought out a consistent position as to how these assumptions and beliefs fit with God and his character, his love for humans, his justice, and what the Bible actually teaches. Those who do try to figure it out frequently get stuck, make little progress, and give up. They end up not thinking or talking at all about the final judgment and punishment, leaving the subjects to Bible scholars and pastors. A large problem is many pastors are reluctant to openly address final judgment and punishment, and like most other Christians avoid the topics or are embarrassed when they are brought up, especially with non-believers.

Those who do venture to discuss the subjects often stumble and contradict themselves like I did. Even worse, some who have strong but misguided beliefs about punishment and the final judgment have generated confusion and even humiliation to the Christian church. We've surely heard a street preacher threaten passersby with eternal hell, but didn't stay long enough to hear the entire sermon because we were too embarrassed to associate ourselves with both the messenger and their message. I remember attending a service in a large church where a visiting missionary was speaking. He told the congregation that those who haven't heard the gospel are lost, and when they die they will burn in hell forever and ever, then insisting that was the main reason we should support missions work. The implication was that if missionaries can't reach the unreached, then those that don't give money to them are guilty of sending people to hell forever. It didn't surprise me at all that his sermon left some confused and others angry and disillusioned.

Too many pastors, Bible teachers, and other Christians rely on their particular church traditions or doctrines when dealing with final judgment and punishment, or simply repeat what they have read or heard from others, but can't defend their view from Scripture. The purpose of *Final Judgment & the Goodness of God* is to examine Scripture to arrive at solidly biblical viewpoints on God's final judgment and punishment. It is for Christians who have a difficult time reconciling their current assumptions about hell with what they know about God's character and love for all people. An understanding of these topics will give them a true perspective and needed confidence so that they will be able to "give the reason for the hope that you have." (1 Peter 3:15)

Before we begin, it is important to remember that the Bible was written to be read and understood by average people. It was not meant only to be studied and explained by highly trained scholars and theologians. The Bible does not consist of elaborate complicated beliefs about God based on the special knowledge and insight of a few learned individuals. *Final Judgment & the Goodness of God* was written knowing that the Bible was written to be read, understood, and applied by anyone who truly wants to know God. The gospels (the books of Matthew, Mark, Luke, and John) in particular were written so the everyday person might believe and find salvation: "But these are written that you may believe that Jesus is the Christ, the Son of God, and that by believing you may have life in his name." (John 20:31) Therefore, any particularly complex theology of judgment and punishment by God should be held suspect.

Final Judgment & the Goodness of God was also created for students of the Bible who desire to understand it, and the topics this book addresses, in more depth. If we hope to make progress in knowing and communicating the truth to others, we cannot laser focus on two or three passages that seem to support a view that we prefer, or take passages out of their proper context to build a theology that was not held by the authors of the Bible. And we certainly cannot just parrot what we have heard from others or stubbornly cling to the traditions of our chosen church. Because of the difficult and significant nature of these subjects, it is vital that we base our inquiry on what Scripture actually says as well as its context, studying it thoroughly and leaving no stone unturned.

Hopefully, *Final Judgment & the Goodness of God* will inspire you to dig deeper into the Bible on your own and come to your own conclusions.

Be bold and unafraid to delve into the Scriptures on a quest to find the answers, however inconvenient they may be. So let's begin, and ask God to lead us as we go.

Chapter 1

God of Love and Justice

In God's dealings with humans, he ceaselessly proves that he is good, loving, and kind toward us. There are countless examples of this in Scripture and throughout history. God shows kindness every day even though most people don't acknowledge his kindness, show gratitude, or even acknowledge his existence. Jesus proclaimed, "He causes his sun to rise on the evil and the good, and sends rain on the righteous and the unrighteous," (Matthew 5:45) and "He is kind to the ungrateful and wicked." (Luke 6:35) I am always amazed at those in our country who have an abundance of food, clothes, potable water, a good home, and air to breathe, yet cannot find much to be thankful for. But the fact these people are allowed to continue their life this way provides inconvertible proof that God is good, loving, and kind because he keeps sending good things to those who don't recognize it.

The Apostle John proclaims, "God is love. Whoever lives in love lives in God, and God in him." (1 John 4:16) Of course, the ultimate proof of God's love for us was shown in sending Christ to Earth to dwell among us and then die in our place to bring us eternal salvation.

At the same time, God has proven himself to be just and fair to all people and also able to give pain, suffering, and difficulty to those who ignore and violate his commands. However, God's justice has not always been evident since he is patient and compassionate and does not punish all wrongdoing in this life immediately or, sometimes, even at all. We do not yet see a world where divine justice has been fully served. This leaves many people to conclude that God does not care about justice, or simply doesn't exist.

After World War Two, for example, people across the globe started to question the existence of God. Many were left in a spiritual vacuum in the wake of the extreme cruelty of Nazi Germany and the great atrocities it committed. In particular, many Jewish people asked, "Where was God during the Holocaust? If there is a God, how could he have allowed this to happen?"

It wasn't easy for Dutch Christian Corrie ten Boom to understand what her Nazi captors had done to her, tormenting her at Ravensbruck and causing the death of her sister Betsy. Ten years after her release, Corrie ran into a woman who refused to look her in the eyes. Confused, she asked about the lady and was told the woman had been a nurse at a concentration camp.

The memories instantly flashed back. Corrie recalled taking Betsy to the infirmary to see that very nurse. Betsy was dying, and the woman had been cruel and sharp-tongued. At that moment, Corrie's hatred returned with a vengeance. Her rage so boiled that she knew of only one thing to do.

"Forgive me," she cried out. "Forgive my hatred, O Lord. Teach me to love my enemies!"

Suddenly, God cooled Corrie's embittered heart, and she felt the rage displaced with a divine love she couldn't explain. Corrie began praying for her, and one day shortly afterward called the hospital where the nurse worked and invited the woman to a meeting at which she was speaking.

The nurse was incredulous. "What?" she replied. "You want me to come?"

"Yes, that is why I called you."

That evening after her talk, Corrie sat down with the nurse and shared how she had come to love God despite the atrocities done to her and to her sister. The woman seemed to thirst for Corrie's quiet, confident words about God's grace—and the former captive led her former captor to salvation through Jesus Christ.

It has been well documented that many Jews actually left their faith because they could not reconcile what happened in Germany with the existence of a God they were taught was good, loving, kind, and a protector of those who believed in him. For those today who do believe in God's existence and love, faith in the justice of God must rest on his promise that he will punish wrongdoing in the future, and vindicate those who have been unjustly wronged like Corrie and the Jews of the Holocaust era. We must be content to accept God's promise in Scripture that he will someday punish all evil and balance the scales of justice. "It is mine to avenge; I will repay." (Deuteronomy 32:35)

For those who struggle with these difficult questions about life and faith, it is vitally important how we approach them. Are we sincerely seeking answers from God and willing to accept his answers, or do our questions about things we don't understand amount to accusations against God?

Scripture declares that God is love. We like this, so much so that many of us feel this is all we need to know about God. However, the English word "love" has morphed over the years and can now mean many things: deep affection, romantic passion, or even endearment toward a place or thing. This means the perception of God's character and attributes will vary from person to person depending on their concept of love. In the minds of many, love excludes punishment of any sort, and if God is a loving God, then he cannot punish people for wrongdoing. Conversely, if God does, in fact, punish people for their sins, then he cannot be loving. It is either love or justice, one or the other. God cannot possess both.

Others who know the Bible understand God to be both loving and just, but conclude that he cannot be both at the same time. When he is punishing he is not being loving, and when he is showing his love he cannot be just. To them, the two are simply incompatible. There is also a trend within some churches that a loving God could never sentence anyone to a final punishment. They view the final judgment is not being final at all, believing God will give everyone opportunities to be saved even after they die.

From Genesis to Revelation, the Lord is revealed as a God of love and justice simultaneously. Since he is unchanging, his attributes do not vary with time or circumstances. Exodus 34:6-7 declares, "The Lord, the Lord, the compassionate and gracious God, slow to anger, abounding in love and faithfulness, maintaining love to thousands, and forgiving wickedness, rebellion and sin. Yet he does not leave the guilty unpunished." (Exodus 34:6-7) We will learn that God does not show love at the expense of justice, nor does he execute justice at the cost of his love. God will punish all sin and rebellion on the final Day of Judgment, and will not negate his love in doing so.

Chapter 2

Salvation by Grace, Judgment by Works

One of the greatest theological debates in the history of the Christian church has been whether we are saved by grace through faith alone or also by works. I remember a conversation I had with Benjamín, a middle-aged man who owned a small ranch and farm in a remote mountain area in Mexico. My wife Nancy and I were there as part of a mission outreach, something we did for eight fulfilling years. As a part of our community development work there, my wife worked as a nutritionist while I utilized my hydrology skills to drill potable water wells and provide safe drinking water for small impoverished communities.

We drilled a well in Benjamín's community, and over the course of time, we became good friends with him. We often talked about the gospel and had come to agreement on many issues in the Bible. One evening after being invited to dinner at his small, rustic ranch house, we had a specific discussion about salvation and forgiveness, and my assertion that we can only receive both through faith in Christ seemed reasonable

5

to Benjamín. He was a humble and gracious man, and a true believer in Christ. Being raised Roman Catholic, though, he had one main objection.

"But we need good deeds also." He expressed this with all seriousness and sincerity, and try as I might, I could not convince him that our good deeds were the *result* of our faith in Christ and love for God, not another ingredient that must be added on to our faith in order to enter heaven. We don't do good works to *become* God's children; the good things that we do show that we *are* his children.

When the great nineteenth-century Bible teacher Charles Spurgeon was a teen, he was asked to preach at his grandfather's church in Suffolk, England. His train was late, though, so his grandfather started the sermon without him. His text was Ephesians 2:8-9: "For it is by grace you have been saved, through faith—and this not from yourselves, it is a gift of God—not by works, so that no one can boast."

Moments later, in walked Charles, and his grandfather stopped and told the congregation, "Here comes my grandson. He can preach the gospel better than I can, but you cannot preach a better gospel, can you, Charles?"

"You are so right, grandfather," he replied, then graciously took the pulpit. As young Charles expounded on the truth of "saved by faith, not by works," his grandfather encouraged him. "Good! Tell them again, Charles. Tell them again!" Ever after, Charles Spurgeon said that whenever he preached from Ephesians 2, he could hear his grandfather's words. "Tell them again!"

It is a wonderful truth—and while I was sure then, and remain certain now, that my statements to Benjamín about salvation through faith in Christ were correct, I realize that I was missing a vital, additional piece during those conversations with him. What about all the passages in the Bible that talk about how we will be judged based on our deeds?

In many Old and New Testament passages we find the same concept: we all must appear before God to give an account of our lives. In 2 Corinthians 5:10, the Apostle Paul declared, "For we must all appear before the judgment seat of Christ, that each one may receive what is due him for the things done while in the body, whether good or bad." Hebrews 9:27 states that we are destined to die once, and after that comes the judgment. In Ecclesiastes 3:17, King Solomon wrote, "God will bring to judgment both the righteous and the wicked." Romans 14:10-12 adds, "For we will all stand before God's judgment seat ... each of us will give an account of himself to God."

Contrary to some popular church theologies, the Bible states that all people will appear before God regardless of their social, religious, age, gender, or spiritual status. Many Christians have no problem with God judging unbelievers by their bad deeds, but think believers should be exempt from such judgment because of God's grace.

Ephesians 2:8-9 clearly states that we are saved by grace through faith, not by our works. However, there are numerous additional references in the Bible to a final judgment where all people, regardless of their stated faith, will appear and be judged by their works. Common arguments stemming from this apparent discrepancy make a case for the believer's exemption from final judgment based on God's grace through the death of Christ. One theology, developed in the twentieth century, holds that all true believers who are resurrected (or "raptured") prior to the millennial reign of Jesus will rule with Christ on Earth until the final judgment, but will not be judged at that judgment.

Yet many key passages from both the Old and New

Testaments agree that both believers and unbelievers will appear before God to give an accounting of their lives on judgment day. Romans 2:5-8 states that God will judge every person according to their deeds. "But because of your stubbornness and your unrepentant heart, you are storing up wrath against yourself for the day of God's wrath, when his righteous judgment will be revealed. God 'will give to each person according to what he has done.' To those who by persistence in doing good seek glory, honor and immortality, he will give eternal life. But for those who are self-seeking and who reject the truth and follow evil, there will be wrath and anger." The "day of God's wrath" must refer to the judgment of all people, both unbelievers and believers, since some receive God's wrath and others receive eternal life. In the Old Testament, Psalms 62:12 likewise declares of the Lord, "Surely you will reward each person according to what he has done." A pattern emerges from these passages. We are saved by grace through faith, but both believers and unbelievers will be judged by our works on judgment day.

The righteous and the wicked

There is a popular belief that we will all be judged by the balance of good deeds versus bad deeds done while living on the Earth. In this view, the fate of people we deem as being evil (such as Hitler or Stalin) is clear. They will go to hell. Likewise, the fate of those we universally recognize as being good is also clear—but many of us fit most everyone else into this group because we believe most people are basically good and thus deserve to go to heaven. This group usually includes our friends, family members, and those we unquestioningly recognize as being good, such as Mother Teresa. But what about those we place somewhere in the middle who are not obviously good or evil? Do they face an uncertain outcome?

Depending on which way the scale tips, they'll be very fortunate and go to heaven or very unfortunate and go to the other place. The sheer uncertainty of this belief is enough to make anyone look for a better way to be saved.

The Bible teaches in many passages that the final judgment will result in blessings for the righteous and punishment for the wicked. These two words, righteous and wicked, are used countless times in both Old and New Testaments. The Old Testament is filled with references to the "righteous" (rendered in the Hebrew as *tsaddiq*), which means just, innocent, or blameless. The New Testament Greek word for righteous, *dikaios,* has the same meaning. Neither word means morally perfect, for no one fits that description except God himself, but they do speak of someone who has been approved by God. *Dikaios* is also used in the New Testament to describe someone who is upright and of good character, such as Joseph (Matthew 1:19). "Wicked" generally refers to those who are ungodly, evil, lawless, or unrepentant. The Hebrew word for wicked is *rasha* and is used in many passages including Genesis 18:23, Isaiah 13:11, and Psalm 75:10. The Greek word for wicked is *poneros* and is also translated "evil" in some passages. A typical use for *poneros* is found in Matthew 13:49-50 in Jesus' parable of the net: "This is how it will be at the end of the age. The angels will come and separate the wicked from the righteous and throw them into the fiery furnace, where there will be weeping and gnashing of teeth." In this passage, the wicked are clearly those who are condemned by God.

A key Old Testament passage that sheds additional light on this subject is Malachi 3:18, where the prophet declares, "And you will again see the distinction between the righteous and the wicked, between those who serve God and those who do not." Simply put, the righteous are those who love and serve God, (not those who are morally perfect or whose good deeds outweigh their bad ones), while the wicked are those who do not love or serve God.

The Apostle Paul brings even more clarity: "For in the gospel a righteousness from God is revealed, a righteousness that is by faith from first to last, just as it is written: 'The righteous will live by faith.'" (Romans 1:17) The term righteous, then, refers to an outward expression of an inward reality, produced primarily by being in a faith relationship with God. People are not righteous within themselves, independently of God.

Therefore, it's evident that being judged according to works does not contradict God's grace because our deeds are evidence of who we really are. Faith in Christ saves us now and for the future—and if we have genuine faith, our lives will demonstrate the reality of that salvation through our actions in service to God. The Day of Judgment will reveal the authenticity of our faith.

The apparent disagreement between Romans 2 (judged by works) and Ephesians 2 (saved by grace) can also be resolved by connecting Paul's teachings to those of Jesus. In Romans 2:7, the Apostle Paul describes those who seek God and his truth, "who by persistence in doing good seek glory, honor and immortality." In Matthew 7:7, Christ gave the promise, "Ask and it will be given to you; seek and you will find; knock and the door will be opened to you." He went on in verse 11 to explain that our heavenly Father is kind and gracious to everyone, giving "good gifts to those who ask him!" These passages reveal that the issue is one of the heart. Those who really want to know God will seek him, and they will find him because he is kind and makes himself abundantly available to those who look for him.

This amazing truth brings to mind the story of a well-known English deist, Anthony Collins of the seventeenth century, who one day crossed paths with a commoner. "Where are you going?" asked Collins.

"To church, sir," the person responded.

"What are you going to do there?"

"To worship God, sir."

Collins pressed, "Is your God a great or a little God?"

"He is both, sir."

Intrigued, he inquired, "How can he be both?"

The commoner smiled. "He is so great, sir, that the heaven of heavens cannot contain him, and so little that he can dwell in my heart."

This great and small God is indeed more than willing to forgive and save those that seek him. Those who don't want to know him will remain in darkness because God doesn't force himself on anyone. The unrepentant, those who are "self-seeking and reject the truth and follow evil" (Romans 2:8) will only receive God's wrath on the Day of Judgment. Because they have rebelled against God with no intention of changing, there is no other option remaining than God's condemnation.

Rewards and condemnation

The fact that the righteous will be rewarded at the judgment for their service to God is demonstrated in the parable of the talents (Matthew 25:14-30). In it, Jesus tells of a master who entrusted various amounts of money (referred to as "talents") to his servants to invest while he went on a journey. Those who invested wisely and received various rates of return were rewarded by the master when he came back home. The master's reply to them was the oft-quoted passage "Well done, good and faithful servant!" The rewards were not described in detail but included being put "in charge of many things" and sharing in the "master's happiness." One can only imagine what this really means for believers who have faithfully served

11

Christ. The story strongly suggests that eternal rewards will involve sharing in God's joy, enjoying his awesome presence, and doing so in a place and position of incredible privilege, for "no eye has seen, no ear has heard, no mind has conceived what God has prepared for those who love him." (1 Corinthians 2:9)

But for the servant who did not invest the money but buried it, the master was angry and called him wicked and lazy. He took the talent from him, gave it to one of the other servants, fired him on the spot, and threw him outside, where he experienced "weeping and gnashing of teeth." (Matthew 25:30) This servant believed that the master was a hard man and someone to be afraid of, so he did not obey the master but hid the talent that was given to him, meaning that it didn't increase in value. In this parable, we should not take the term "servant" to mean "servant of God," nor should we interpret the wicked servant as a metaphor for disobedient Christians. Jesus' story simply portrays servants of a household wherein the faithful were commended and the lazy were punished. It clearly speaks of the righteous who gain rewards and the wicked who receive condemnation at the final judgment. More specifically, the wicked and lazy servant represents the unrighteous who do not love God and who grossly misjudge his character. They believe God to be harsh and vindictive and someone to avoid, not someone to please and serve.

It is not clear whether the unrighteous will be given varying degrees of condemnation at the final judgment, but some Bible commentators believe that they will. This is based on Mark 12:40 ("These men will be punished most severely."), Luke 6:38 ("With the measure you use, it will be measured to you."), and Luke 12:47-48 (describing servants who will be beaten with many or few blows). Some also believe, on the basis of the Luke 12 passage, that the wicked will undergo differing amounts of suffering before being given their final punishment.

Another of Christ's parables, that of the sheep and the goats (Matthew 25:31-46) also addresses rewards. Jesus talks about a single, individual judgment event where both believers and unbelievers are present to be judged. The believers are rewarded for their faithful service to God, and even if they weren't aware of what they were doing at the time, Christ confirms that they were indeed serving God as they loved and met the needs of others. The unbelievers, conversely, are punished for their lack of response to opportunities to serve God. They likewise may not have been aware of what they were doing or not doing, but Christ assures them that they did not serve God because they did not love and serve others. A key to understanding this parable is the simple concept that God wants us to love all people because *he* loves all people. If we love others as he loves them, then we are accurately representing who God is to the world. This parable also reveals that at the final judgment God will not consider what a person says but what a person *does*, which is a more accurate reflection of that individual's heart. In an ingenious way, God has hidden his image in every human being so that our love for God is proven by our care for others who, like us, are made in his image and in need of God's love.

The Bible affirms that those who seek God will find God, live in service to God, and then be rewarded for their deeds at the final judgment—while those who do not seek God will not find or serve him, and therefore will be given condemnation at the judgment. There is no conflict between the salvation by grace spoken of in Ephesians 2 and the judgment by works spoken of in Romans 2. Those saved by faith are God's people who live out their faith through their service to God and others, while those who are not saved show that fact in their lives and actions. Ephesians 2 addresses the means of salvation. Romans 2 teaches the results of salvation.

The Waldensians' faith and works

Peter Waldo was a wealthy merchant who lived in the twelfth century. Being a committed Christian, he became disillusioned with his wealthy lifestyle, gave away his fortunes, and lived a life of simplicity and devotion to God. He eventually became the leader of a movement of Christians called the Waldensians, who are thought by many to be the early forerunners of the Reformation. They believed strongly that their faith should be based only on the Bible and its teachings, not the doctrine of a specific church. Waldo had the New Testament translated into the common language of the day (Provencal) and distributed it so that the common person could read it or hear it themselves. Laypeople preached from the Bible at their gatherings, held usually in the home. They believed unwaveringly that the source of their salvation was the atoning death of Christ rather than the sacraments of the Roman Catholic Church. However, they also had a strong belief that true faith results in a life of devotion, good works, and non-retaliation against their enemies. Their simple faith and love for their neighbors caused the movement to spread rapidly throughout Europe.

The Waldensians naturally came into conflict with the Roman Catholic Church because they did not accept the authority of the Pope or Church leadership. They were therefore declared to be heretics and were mercilessly persecuted by the Inquisition. Many from the Church accepted the Waldensians and made peace with them, but the Inquisition continued to attack. Several massacres occurred where unspeakable atrocities were committed by those acting under the authority of the Church. Waldensian worship was held in secret and their preachers travelled undercover from town to town. When the

Inquisition gave the Waldensians an ultimatum to renounce their faith or be forced from their homes, most chose the latter. Many settled in the Alpine valleys of the Piedmont but were eventually found and persecuted anew. Over several centuries, thousands of Waldensians were beaten, tortured, buried alive, and burned at the stake. Their women were raped, and their homes were set ablaze—yet they were not deterred from their faith, even though their numbers significantly decreased and their churches almost disappeared.

Although we cannot sit in God's judgment seat, from our viewpoint it's accurate to say that the early Waldensians had a saving faith that resulted in good works, while their persecutors demonstrated they did not. We don't know much about the Waldensians' early leaders, so their faith and courage have gone largely unnoticed over time. However, I won't be surprised if many of them are counted among the great people of faith on the Day of Judgment. The Waldensians ultimately survived, later came to embrace the Reformation, and many Waldensian churches exist today in Europe, the United States, and South America. In 2015, Pope Francis formally asked forgiveness from the Waldensian Christians for the atrocities committed against them by the Church in a most fitting conclusion to this dark episode of church history.

In his discourse on the tree and its fruit in Matthew 7, Jesus warned that not everyone who claims to have faith will enter the kingdom of heaven, but "only he who does the will of my Father who is in heaven." (Matthew 7:21) It will not be what a person says or claims on that great day, but what a person has done that will indicate his love for God. Many will be outraged when Jesus rejects their claim to faith on judgment day, but their actions and the way they lived will prove they were not his followers. Jesus' words to them will be direct. "I never knew you. Away from me, you evildoers." (Matthew 7:23)

15

These unfortunate souls will include all those who persecuted others in the name of their religion, as well as the great and powerful who oppressed the helpless for personal gain or even for the sake of what they thought was a good cause. For them, the tables will be turned when they find themselves standing before the almighty God to give an account.

In Matthew 12, Jesus again brought up a tree and its fruit when, speaking to the Pharisees, he warned, "A tree is recognized by its fruit. You brood of vipers, how can you who are evil say anything good? For out of the overflow of the heart the mouth speaks." (Matthew 12:33-34) The true character of a person is revealed by what they talk about. Jesus then added this astonishing statement: "But I tell you that men will have to give account on the day of judgment for every careless word they have spoken. For by your words you will be acquitted, and by your words you will be condemned." (Matthew 12:36-37) From this warning we learn a vital truth: what we say in this life discloses our actual thoughts and desires, and therefore, who we really are—and it is by these words that we will be judged, not by the claims we make or the words we utter in our own defense on judgment day.

King Solomon concludes Ecclesiastes with this timeless and convicting exhortation: "Now all has been heard; here is the conclusion of the matter: Fear God and keep his commandments, for this is the whole duty of man. For God will bring every deed into judgment, including every hidden thing, whether it is good or evil." (Ecclesiastes 12:13-14)

So, if we are indeed saved by grace but judged by works, exactly how many judgments are there? When does judgment take place? And what kind of attitude should we have toward God's judgment?

Chapter 3

One, Two, or Three Judgments?

"**W**hy would God want to judge anyone?" Chen asked my wife, Nancy, after reading a passage about the final judgment. They had been studying the Bible together regularly for quite some time at a quaint, nonsectarian gathering place on the University of Arizona campus, and sat across from each other at a table in the small, brightly-lit meeting room. "Isn't judging wrong?" Chen asked, then asserted, "Jesus said we should not judge."

Chen was Chinese and a typical post-modern millennial student who didn't like absolutes or being told what to do. Although she was a Christian, for her and others like her, judging someone is anathema; it's the equivalent of an attack and something you just don't do under any circumstances. While Chen did not know the English language well enough to know there are different meanings and applications of the word "judge," she still maintained the aversion to the word shared by many others in our culture that judging is wrong—and that if God was truly a loving God, he would not judge anyone, either.

I have encountered the same perspective in my conversations with both international students and those from

American culture. Yet while *we* are not to take the Lord's place in judgment of others, God, as the sovereign Lord and Creator, does have the right to judge those he created.

The word "judgment" in the Bible can refer to the final judgment as well as to a punishment in this present life. There are many times recorded in the Old Testament when God has already judged individuals, groups, or even nations as punishment for sins. There are also references in the Bible to future judgments of God such as those in the book of Revelation. In these cases, judgment is a verdict by God over sin and a resulting punishment in this present life, whereas the final judgment takes place at the end of time when God judges all of humanity.

Believers throughout the ages have developed theologies of different levels and categories of the final judgment. Some are based on more literal interpretations, while others are more allegorical. But throughout the Bible, the portrayal of the final judgment is similar to that of an earthly court of law, where people stand before the judge, an assessment is given, a verdict is decided, and the judged is either acquitted or punished. Some verses in the Bible describe the process of appearing before God to be judged. Other references emphasize the pronouncement of a verdict (such as condemnation) or describe the punishment that results for the unrepentant (destruction, being thrown into the lake of fire, and perishing). In many portrayals, rewards are given to the acquitted or the faithful. Because the images in these various references are different, some claim they describe entirely separate judgment events. The three events commonly cited are the "judgment seat of Christ," the "sheep and the goats" judgment, and the "great white throne" judgment.

The "judgment seat of Christ" judgment is described in 2 Corinthians 5:10. "For we must all appear before the judgment seat of Christ, that each one may receive what is due him for the things done while in the body, whether good or bad." This passage is cited by many as applying only to believers when Christ will reward each for their service to him. The "sheep and the goats" judgment is from Matthew 25 as mentioned in the previous chapter. "When the Son of Man comes in his glory, and all the angels with him, he will sit on his throne in heavenly glory. All the nations will be gathered before him, and he will separate the people from one another as a shepherd separates the sheep from the goats. He will put the sheep on his right and the goats on his left." (Matthew 25:31-33) According to some, this judgment occurs immediately after the great tribulation period and before the millennial reign of Christ. Others believe it occurs after the millennial reign is completed. The "great white throne" judgment refers to the event portrayed in Revelation 20:11-12. "Then I saw a great white throne and him who was seated on it. Earth and sky fled from his presence, and there was no place for them. And I saw the dead, great and small, standing before the throne, and books were opened. Another book was opened, which is the book of life. The dead were judged according to what they had done as recorded in the books." Some assert that only unbelievers appear at this judgment while believers are exempt. Others claim the "great white throne" judgment and the "sheep and the goats" judgment are the same but separate from the "judgment seat of Christ."

A logical look at the judgment events

This view of separate final judgment events, one for believers and another for unbelievers, is attractive to some because it fits into a particular end-times theology, but it is speculative. Such an approach to biblical interpretation might appear to solve problems and explain discrepancies by saying the passages refer to completely different events. However, this approach makes it difficult to reconcile these passages to others that speak to a broader scope and bigger picture of God's plan for humanity. To establish that these are different judgment events, we have to explain how these events intertwine, who is present at each, what is the impact for the individual believer and unbeliever, and when each event occurs. The labyrinth of events and concepts becomes complex and burdensome to correlate, especially when parallel scriptures don't seem to agree on all points.

One theory is that the final judgments for believers and unbelievers actually occur at different moments but relatively close to each other within the "end times" that may span a number of years. In this view, the *exact* occurrence of each of the events is not important, but just the fact that they occur when God settles accounts with all of humanity. That both the Apostles Paul and Peter seem to lump the events of the end times together in some passages seems to support this. Regardless, it is more logical to conclude there is one final judgment event where all people who have died are judged before entering their final and eternal state, and that the vast majority of references to judgment day in the New Testament refer to this single event. For example, the judgment event in Revelation 20 is quite similar to the "sheep and the goats" event of Matthew 25. Also, Paul also does not distinguish between the "judgment seat of Christ" he described in 2 Corinthians 5 and the "sheep and the goats" judgment Jesus declared. He only referenced one event when speaking about the subject of final judgment.

An unbiased reading of the phrase, "we must all appear" in 2 Corinthians 5:10 strongly suggests that it speaks of all people and not just believers. Many commentators use the rarity of term "judgment seat of Christ" as proof that the 2

Corinthians 5 event is a separate judgment event, but this is scant evidence. It is probable that this is just the term that the apostle chose to use for the final judgment of all humanity. In Romans 14:10, Paul used similar wording when he wrote, "For we will all stand before God's judgment seat," followed by a quote from Isaiah 45:23: "'As surely as I live' says the Lord, 'every knee will bow before me; every tongue will confess to God.'" The clear context of the Isaiah passage is salvation and the judgment of everyone in the world and not just believers, as shown by the passage preceding it: "Turn to me and be saved, all you ends of the earth; for I am God, and there is no other." (Isaiah 45:22) Additionally, when Paul is preaching to the Athenians about idolatry, he stated, "In the past God overlooked such ignorance, but now he commands all people everywhere to repent. For he has set a day when he will judge the world with justice by the man he has appointed. He has given proof of this to all men by raising him from the dead." (Acts 17:30-31) Paul said that Christ, "the man he has appointed," will judge all people at one great event.

In his parables and teachings, Jesus does not talk about two judgments, but only one. If there were two separate judgments, one for unbelievers and another for believers, then Jesus would've said so clearly and likely defined them. This is evident when Jesus described the judgment that will fall on unrepentant people in the towns of Korazin and Bethsaida as recorded in Matthew 11:22. He declared, "But I tell you, it will be more bearable for Tyre and Sidon on the day of judgment than for you." Regarding Capernaum, he added in verse 24, "But I tell you that it will be more bearable for Sodom on the day of judgment than for you." Similarly, in Matthew 12:41, Jesus described the judgment on the generation of his time that were unfaithful to God. "The men of Nineveh will stand up at the judgment with this generation and condemn it; for they repented at the preaching of Jonah, and now one greater than Jonah is here." Jesus made no distinction between the "judgment" of Matthew 12, the "day of judgment" of Matthew 11, or between any of his other references to the final judgment found throughout the gospels.

Giving of rewards

In Matthew 16:27, Jesus proclaimed of himself, "For the Son of Man is going to come in his Father's glory with his angels, and then he will reward each person according to what he has done." The context of this verse is obedience to Christ's call to faithful discipleship, and Jesus could be referring to a time immediately after his second return to the earth, when he gives rewards to his followers for faithful service and punishes those that opposed him during the great tribulation period. If this is the case, then the final judgment does not occur at this time, but only a giving of rewards to God's people who are alive at the time of Christ's return. However, the same phrasing of coming "in his Father's glory with his angels" is similarly used in the parable of the "sheep and the goats," which almost certainly refers to the final judgment since the unrighteous are thrown into the eternal fire. These verses illustrate the difficulty of conclusively proving or disproving that there are separate judgments for believers and the wicked. While the purpose of *Final Judgment & the Goodness of God* is not to answer all the questions about the second coming and the millennial reign of Christ, Matthew 16:27 more likely correlates with the second coming of Christ and the events in Revelation 14 that will be examined later in this book.

Years ago, my wife and I hosted a Bible study at our home. It attracted a wide array of people from diverse backgrounds, including some with disabilities. One Christian woman who attended for a while was Sigrid, who had an incurable neurological disease that eventually caused complete blindness. Sigrid knew her Bible well and always made sure that our discussions were on track. But, being blind, she needed considerable assistance to be picked up and led out of her home, driven to the study, and then back home when we were done. This added considerable stress for us to provide this transportation because of our full time jobs. One evening, as I was driving to pick her up, I started to complain. But then something reminded me of words of Jesus from his parable of the "sheep and the goats," where he said, "Whatever you did for one of the least of these brothers of mine, you did for me." (Matthew 25:40) Immediately, I was overwhelmed with gratitude as I realized what a great privilege it was to help our sister Sigrid. We were serving not just her, but Jesus our Lord. Sigrid's disease overtook her some years later and she passed away, but I and the many others who knew and served her know that we will see her on that great final judgment day when he declares, "Whatever you did ... you did for me."

That time of rewards for Sigrid and all other believers is also referred to in Revelation 11:18, where the 24 elders who are worshiping God say of the Lord, "The nations were angry; and your wrath has come. The time has come for judging the dead, and for rewarding your servants the prophets and your saints and those who reverence your name." The elders in this scene are describing the time of final judgment that includes both the judging of the dead and the giving of rewards for those who have served God. In summary, those who love God and believe the gospel will have salvation, plus whatever rewards that are coming to them for faithful service, while those who do not love God and refuse to believe will have condemnation at the judgment, plus a final and irreversible punishment.

The believers' assessment

If believers will also be judged, then what is the purpose of this judgment and how will they be judged?

Believers in Christ are children of God by adoption (Ephesians 1:5) and at the final judgment they are not condemned along with the unbelieving world. Christians will not be punished along with the unrighteous, "for God did not appoint us to suffer wrath but to receive salvation through our Lord Jesus Christ." (1 Thessalonians 5:9) When believers in this life commit sin, God, out of his fatherly love, disciplines them as his children. (Hebrews 12: 5-6) But the Lord treats the wicked differently. They do not receive discipline in this life for the sins they commit but receive justice and punishment at the final judgment.

But some believers confuse their status as children of God to therefore give them an exemption at the final judgment, concluding they cannot be "judged" because they are already saved. In addition, some churches teach that the only issue of importance is whether we are saved or not, because once we are saved, then we are going to heaven so nothing else matters. For believers, however, the final judgment will not be a punishment, but rather more of an assessment, a time of proving, and a moment of purifying.

In 1 Corinthians, Paul discusses this assessment of each believer's work on earth, stating that if their work is not built with durable materials, it will be burnt up. "If any man builds on this foundation using gold, silver, costly stones, wood, hay, or straw, his work will be shown for what it is, because the Day will bring it to light. It will be revealed with fire, and the fire will test the quality of each man's work. If what he has built survives, he will receive his reward. If it is burned up, he will suffer loss; he himself will be saved, but only as one escaping through the flames." (1 Corinthians 3:12-15) This passage delivers the strong message that the believer's judgment will consist of the receiving of rewards for enduring work, but also an experience of loss for actions and work that did not serve his eternal purposes and thus will not survive the judgment. These will be "burned up," and for this the believer will "suffer loss." As a broad statement, we could say that only that which is *eternal* will survive that great day. Noteworthy is the fact that Paul only uses the term "the Day" to identify this event. It's brevity, without any explanation, strongly suggests that Paul assumed that his readers were fully aware what he was referring to: the final judgment day that he references in all of his other letters.

So what is the purpose of the believer's judgment? God's purposes for judging the believer on the final day is to certify and affirm their status as his children, to evaluate the results of their faith while on Earth, and then to reward them for faithful service. How will the Christian be judged? By an assessment of our service to him which culminates in the destruction of work which was combustible and not fit for God's kingdom, and then rewarding work that was enduring and *did* advance his kingdom.

From this we understand the importance of building the foundation of our lives not on wood, hay, or straw, but only on that which will endure the fire—because we know we will one day be judged by the Lord. Some people struggle with this and minimize its importance. Then there's Clay Shiver, who, according to author Ken Walker,[1] was a highly-regarded college football athlete at Florida State University. One magazine even wanted to name him to their prestigious preseason All-America football squad. It's an honor that meant the nation's sportswriters considered him to be one of the premier football players in the country. Such publicity can lead to

---

1   Ken Walker, "Ordinary Heroes," *Christian Reader*, Sept/Oct 1995.

a multimillion dollar contract from a team in the National Football League.

But Shiver had higher values and priorities. Because that magazine was *Playboy*, he turned down their selection. "Clay didn't want to embarrass his mother and grandmother by appearing in the magazine or give old high school friends an excuse to buy that issue," said Walker.

Shiver further explained his decision by quoting Luke 12:48: "From everyone who has been given much, much will be demanded; and from the one who has been entrusted with much, much more will be asked."

Shiver went on to play for four years in the NFL and then coach high school football in Florida. Of his decision to reject *Playboy*, he added, "I don't want to let anyone down, and number one on that list is God." Clay wanted to remove from his life any wood, hay, or straw that could in the end be burned up on that great day.

Of course, the lives of most believers are full of pursuits and interests such as hobbies, sports, and music, which certainly bring untold enjoyment to life. Most of these are spiritually and morally neutral in themselves. Will these works also be burned up? The answer is: yes and no. We should acknowledge that our earthly pursuits and interests themselves will not go with us beyond the grave; they will be swallowed up by the much greater glory we will experience as we enter the presence of God. But earthly pursuits can be a conduit for the glory of God and provide a Christian witness as we meet people with like interests. If we allow Christ to show himself as we live our lives, then in the midst of our activities and pursuits there will be eternal effects that *will* survive the Day of Judgment.

In 1 Corinthians 4, the Apostle Paul follows up his discussion about wood, hay, and straw with the following: "My conscience is clear, but that does not make me innocent. It is the Lord who judges me. Therefore judge nothing before the appointed time; wait till the Lord comes. He will bring to light what is hidden in darkness and will expose the motives of men's hearts. At that time each will receive his praise from God." (1 Corinthians 4:4-5) The use of the phrases "appointed time" and "wait till the Lord comes" seem to refer to both the second coming of Christ and the final judgment, and the details of the exact timing of these events is not important to Paul since they are described as one event. More importantly, Paul believed that his service to God came out of pure motives, so he didn't want to presume that all his work was going to remain intact after the judgment. Even though he is reckoned by many Christians as the greatest of the apostles, Paul still acknowledged that some of his work may not survive the great day.

How much more, then, should we prepare for that day? And how much more should we consider eliminating those substandard materials—the wood, hay, and straw; anything that doesn't serve God's eternal purposes—from our lives now so that we won't have to watch them burn up?

Chapter 4

How Can God Judge Those Who Haven't Heard?

One evening at the international student ministry where I taught, a young man named Qiang came to me after class with a question. He was a "seeker" who had already heard many teachings about Christ and the salvation that he brought for us through his death and resurrection. Qiang remained curious enough to keep attending the fellowship on a regular basis but had not come to faith in Jesus.

Before asking his question, Qiang revealed to me that his father in China had cancer and was not expected to live much longer. He also told me that his father had never heard the message of the gospel, but Qiang believed him to be a good person.

He then asked, "Will my father go to heaven?"

The question caught me off guard. I thought, *How do I respond in a way that won't push him away from God?* Just as I had with Di Ya, I answered the best that I could, telling him that God is just and his judgments are fair. But, also as I had with Di Ya, I discerned that my response, though truthful, was not satisfying for Qiang. Not only did it not give him clarity about his father's eternal destiny, he was a bright student pursuing a doctorate in physics and therefore would not accept anything he deemed to be illogical, irrational, or unjust.

In the end, my reply may have provided some comfort for Qiang, but no real guidance one way or the other. Unfortunately, before I was able to fully study this subject to where I could give Qiang a better answer, he stopped attending the ministry meetings, finished his studies, and returned to China to be present when his father died.

Most people born to this world are like Qiang's father. They have not heard the gospel of Jesus clearly explained to them, and the vast majority do not know that there is such an event as the final judgment. Those who have heard may not believe in it or associate their behavior or way of life as anything deserving of a final punishment, much less a punishment called hell. It does no good to say that they *should* know because most people on Earth are simply ignorant of these realities. Many, in fact, do not consciously reject God's rule in their lives. It simply doesn't cross their minds that their lives or behavior should be governed by God, even if they believe in his existence. This is because the great majority of humanity lives under spiritual deception from Satan and are mostly ignorant of God's ways. As 1 John 5:19 asserts, "The whole world is under the control of the evil one."

This does not mean, though, that those who have not heard the gospel are somehow exempt from judgment. But it presents a real dilemma. If God is to judge the world, how can he hold a person responsible for something he has never heard? Are we to conclude that *all* those who are spiritually ignorant will receive God's anger and punishment at the final judgment?

Some Protestant denominations have responded to this question by teaching that anyone who has not responded favorably to the spoken message of the gospel by a Christian pastor or evangelist, and then been baptized, will be condemned at the final judgment and punished forever. This is based on what seems to them a logical sequence of the following Bible verse segments: "All have sinned," (Romans 3:23); "No one comes to the Father except through me," (John 14:6); "Whoever believes and is baptized will be saved, but whoever does not believe will be condemned," (Mark 16:16); and, "If anyone's name was not found written in the book of life, he was thrown into the lake of fire." (Revelation 20:15) The Roman Catholic Church maintains that there is an intermediate condition, called "Limbo," for those who are not explicitly Christian. This temporary state was reserved for the just who died before the coming of Jesus, but whose sins could not be forgiven until the work of Christ was completed. Some Catholic theologians also believe in an interim "Limbo of the Infants" which provides a means for unbaptized infants to be saved.

On the other hand, there are those who believe God gives unbelievers a "second chance" to hear and respond to the gospel after they die. They cite 1 Peter 3:18-19 to support this belief. Speaking of Jesus, Peter wrote, "He was put to death in the body but made alive by the Spirit, through whom he also went and preached to the spirits in prison who disobeyed long ago when God waited patiently in the days of Noah while the ark was being built." Commentators provide various explanations of this passage, including the view that it refers to Christ preaching to those in a temporary prison either before or possibly after his resurrection. But many believe that was a one-time event, affecting only those who were disobedient when Noah lived. Later in the same epistle, Peter spoke about those who choose a destructive path in life: "But they will have to give account to him who is ready to judge the living and the dead. For this is the reason the gospel was preached even to those who are now dead, so that they might be judged according to men in regard to the body, but live according to God in regard to the spirit." (1 Peter 4:5-6) The context of Peter's discussion is obviously final judgment, but most commentators interpret this to mean that the gospel had been preached to people who died later ("now" is not present in the Greek), not those who were dead at the time the preaching occurred. It is not clear, then, that the 1 Peter passages can be applied universally to all people, so it is doubtful that they teach the doctrine of a "second chance."

On the far end of the spectrum is the belief of "universalism." It states that if a person is sincere, God will accept them no matter what they believe or which religion they claim. The "Christian" form of universalism holds that God will restore all humanity, the righteous and the wicked, to himself after the final judgment and all will be saved. However, there is no support for either of these views in the many Bible passages reviewed in this book.

Judged by how they responded while they were alive

So how can God hold someone responsible for something they have never heard? The answer is that he will judge people by how they responded to the light and revelation they were given *while living on Earth*. While some people have been given the specific revelation of the message of the gospel (John 3:16), all people who have lived in various places around the world throughout history have been given the general revelation of God's nature and eternal power (Romans 1:20-25), so they "are without excuse" (verse 20) and can respond to him in some way. Those who "worshiped and served created things rather than the Creator" (practiced idolatry) proved that they were not responding to the general revelation that reveals the true God, but preferred a false created god limited to the physical world. Likewise, all have been given a conscience to recognize their moral obligation to him (Romans 2:5-16).

In Romans 2:7, the Apostle Paul wrote, "To those who by persistence in doing good seek glory, honor and immortality, he will give eternal life," Paul later stated, "(Indeed when the Gentiles, who do not have the law, do by nature things required by the law, they are a law for themselves, even though they do not have the law, since they show that the requirements of the law are written on their hearts, their consciences also bearing witness, and their thoughts now accusing, now even defending them.) This will take place on the day when God will judge men's secrets through Jesus Christ, as my gospel declares." Clearly, Paul declares here that the Gentiles (non-Jews) who do not have the Scripture still have an opportunity to respond to God's grace and find salvation if they seek the truth—all written within the context of how God will judge all of humanity. Even more, when they respond positively to the Lord, they will be given eternal life on the final Day of Judgment when "God will judge men's secrets." This phrase shows that he will judge what is hidden in the heart of each person, whether or not they truly sought him or responded to his revelation. As the author of Psalm 44:20-21 declared, "If we had forgotten the name of our God or spread out our hands to a foreign god, would not God have discovered it, since he knows the secrets of the heart?" The "secrets of the heart" are things that only God can know: the thoughts that inhabit our minds and our inward desires which motivate the actions that we take.

The Apostle John addressed this topic. "This is the verdict: Light has come into the world, but men loved darkness instead of light because their deeds were evil. Everyone who does evil hates the light, and will not come into the light for fear that his deeds will be exposed. But whoever lives by the truth comes into the light, so that it may be seen plainly that what he has done has been done through God." (John 3:19-21) Those who do not seek God will move away from the light, while those who seek the Lord will move toward it—and God will supply as much light and revelation as the seeker desires. Scripture also makes clear that those the Lord punishes are those that "refused to love the truth and so be saved." (2 Thessalonians 2:10)

Of course, there are many who believe they are good because they do good things and are kind to other people, but this in itself does not bring salvation. It is entirely possible that people who appear good outwardly are actually selfish and arrogant on the inside. There are undoubtedly many "good" and "kind" people in the world, both religious and non-religious, but their actions in this life will amount to nothing before God's judgment if they do not seek the Lord or love him.

It truly comes down to what we desire in our hearts. If it's the truth, God is more than willing to provide it. If it's not the truth, God will not force it upon us, but he will also not allow us to avoid the consequences of our choice.

God's transcendency

Christians believe that God is transcendent, meaning he is not subject to the limitations of the material universe because he created the physical world and so is not a part of it. By nature and by definition, God is not physically observable and is therefore invisible. Although we cannot see physical "proof" of God, we do have the many evidences of the existence and nature of God in the created universe. These include the awe-inspiring infinite power and beauty found in the cosmos; the complexity, order, and uniform behavior found in atomic structure and the crystal structure of minerals; the incredible complexity and function found in living things; and the intelligence and creativity found in human beings. We can also conclude that the Creator and Source of all these things must be greater than the things he created, including people. Therefore, if we possess intellect, volition, individuality, emotion, and creativity, then we know that God also possesses these attributes, but to an infinite degree.

These evidences serve as pointers and signs of the existence of a transcendent Creator for the seeker who has an honest heart and sincere desire to know the truth. The cynic, however, will reject these evidences since his heart and mind have unconsciously, and sometimes intentionally, established an unattainably high threshold for belief. As a student in my moral philosophy class at the University of Arizona in the late 1970s, my lecturer was a dedicated atheist, a Marxist, and an advocate of complete moral and sexual "freedom." Most of his students admired him for being progressive and avant-garde, and he took particular pride in putting forth arguments against God, relishing the opportunity to ridicule anyone who disagreed with him. His argument against a transcendent God went something like this: "God is like a little green man in a watch, but he won't ever let you find him because he goes away at the very instant you open up the watch." In other words, he maintained that Christians believe in something that doesn't exist, but they continue to believe in spite of the fact that it always goes away when they look for it or start to examine it.

Believers in God know the exact opposite is true. God actually reveals himself when we look for him. When I challenged my lecturer's simplistic logic in the classroom, I was rewarded with a grade of C for the class. However, being a young enthusiastic Christian, I took it as a privilege to have paid a price for my faith, however small it was. After the semester was over, I paid him a visit. As I stepped into his office, he immediately went on the defensive, thinking I was going to challenge the grade he gave me. However, my purpose was to engage him in a conversation about God. After a few minutes of getting nowhere, I gave him a piece of gospel literature, which he ridiculed, and we said our goodbyes. Walking down the echoing corridor, Psalm 14:1 came to mind. "The fool says in his heart, 'There is no God.'"

Salvation by faith revealed in the Old Testament

Some might object to God giving salvation to those that only have general revelation ("to those who by persistence in doing good seek glory, honor, and immortality, he will give eternal life"), asking, "Is that not salvation by works?" It is absolutely *not* salvation by works, any more than the salvation of those in Old Testament times was by works, since these believers did not yet have the specific revelation of the full gospel message either. Their salvation, just like ours, would be by faith in and obedience to the revelation that God gave them at that time.

Two great examples of this are Enoch and Abraham. It was said of Enoch that God "took him away" to heaven without dying because he "walked with God." (Genesis 5:24) The book of Hebrews elaborates, "For before he was taken, he was commended as one who pleased God. And without faith it is impossible to please God, because anyone who comes to him must believe that he exists and that he rewards those who earnestly seek him." (Hebrews 11:5-6) Enoch knew God existed even though he couldn't see him, and this faith compelled Enoch to devoutly search for him. Looking for the Lord consistently throughout his earthly life, Enoch was provided with an extraordinary knowledge of God, and he learned to love the Lord, follow him, and walk with him. God gladly provided Enoch with what his heart desired, a close relationship with his Creator. God eventually took Enoch into his eternal presence so that the relationship could be even closer.

Abraham, who "believed the Lord" and it was "credited it to him as righteousness," (Genesis 15:6) placed his faith in God's promise of a future blessing, that he was going to be the father of many nations, and that all nations were going to be blessed through him. Although the fulfilment of that promise began with the birth of Abraham's son Isaac, the complete fulfillment was still around 2,000 years away. The full scope of the promise, therefore, was not completely clear to Abraham at that time—since God's intention was to ultimately bless the world through the coming of Christ, who was the complete fulfillment of the promise. Yet that did not prevent Abraham from believing, and his faith was still "credited" to him as righteousness; in other words, it was a saving faith.

All who seek him find him

Much later, God told the Israelites through Moses that they were going to be scattered to live among the Gentile nations if they were unfaithful to him. But then he added, "If from there you seek the Lord your God, you will find him if you look for him with all your heart and with all your soul." (Deuteronomy 4:29) The Lord provided a way back to him, even when they were far from their homeland. Although this promise applied mainly to Israel, is it not also true that anyone, Jews and non-Jews alike, can find God if they seek him and look for him with all their heart and soul?

In Matthew 12:41-42, Jesus spoke of the people of Nineveh who will "stand up at the judgment with this generation and condemn it; for they repented at the preaching of Jonah, and now one greater than Jonah is here. The Queen of the South will rise at the judgment with this generation and condemn it;

for she came from the ends of the earth to listen to Solomon's wisdom, and now one greater than Solomon is here." A significant point not often recognized from this passage is that both the men of Nineveh and the Queen of the South were Gentiles who did not have a complete revelation of God, but they responded to what was shown to them. The strong implication was that they therefore experienced a saving faith, even though they had far less information about God than the Jews who did not repent at the preaching of Jesus himself.

Others that didn't hear the full message of the gospel but responded positively to the light that was given include the Magi (Matthew 2:1-12), Simeon (Luke 2:25-32), Anna (Luke 2: 37-38), the man healed from demon possession (Luke 8:26-39), the leper who returned to give praise (Luke 17:11-19), and the thief on the cross (Luke 23:40-43). Although these people lived during the time of Christ, there are many more examples throughout the Bible, and the closer we look, the more we will find.

In his address to the people of Lystra, Paul said God "has not left himself without testimony: He has shown kindness by giving you rain from heaven and crops in their seasons; he provides you with plenty of food and fills your hearts with joy." (Acts 14:17) God has provided a testimony of his love and kindness to all who live on the Earth. Later in Acts, in his address to the Athenians, Paul added, "From one man he made every nation of men, that they should inhabit the whole earth; and he determined the times set for them and the exact places where they should live. God did this so that men would seek him and perhaps reach out for him and find him, though he is not far from each one of us." (Acts 17:26-27) It's clear that Paul says the Gentiles, who had no Jewish background, could find God if they truly looked for him, and that the Lord is not deliberately trying to hide from people, but wants all to know him and come to salvation. To Timothy he wrote unambiguously, "God our Savior, who wants all men to be saved and to come to a knowledge of the truth." (1 Timothy 2:3-4)

Author Don Richardson[1] gives the account of Pachacuti, one of the greatest of Incan rulers, who reigned from 1438 to 1471 A.D. This man was originally dedicated to the worship of the sun god Inti. Sun worship was mandatory for all people in the Incan empire and was the official state religion, complete with elaborate temples and an order of priests to perform the prescribed rituals. But there came a time when Pachacuti questioned the validity of sun god worship. Eventually, he rejected it altogether, reasoning that the sun changes, clouds can dim its light, and its path is set and predetermined by a higher law; therefore, Inti cannot be the true God. He came to the realization that he had been worshipping a physical thing as the Creator.

Even greater, though, was the next conclusion reached by this leader who was truly looking for God. Previously, his father had a dream in which a deity named Viracocha appeared to him as the Creator of all things. He then researched back into the ancient traditions of Incan culture and found that Viracocha was once worshipped long ago but had gone into obscurity. In the traditional belief, Viracocha was thought of as ancient, remote, and supreme, the uncreated Creator of all things. He was also thought to be the very principle of life, the bringer of peace and order, the judge of the actions of humans, and one who can help people overcome their evil tendencies.

From these attributes, it is evident that the true Creator God had revealed himself to someone in the Incan civilization long before, and the tradition and story had survived, although dimly. Pachacuti concluded that this Creator God was certainly worth worshipping and called a council of the

---

1   Don Richardson, *Eternity in Their Hearts*, Baker Publishing Group, March 2006.

priests, commanding that only Viracocha was to be worshipped as Creator while Inti was to be respected only as a fellow created entity. The priests were divided; many accepted Pachacuti's revelation of a Creator God, but others did not and were enraged. This forced Pachacuti into a compromise: to prevent social upheaval, he deemed that only the upper classes could worship Viracocha, but the lower classes, who were accustomed to sun worship, could continue with their traditional religion.

When the Spanish conquistadors overran the Incans less than 100 years later, the upper classes were exterminated, the memory and worship of Viracocha were lost, and the common people were left in the spiritual darkness of idolatry. Yet Pachacuti's seeking heart and courage is to be remembered with admiration—and as evidence of Paul's assertion that anyone can find God, even in the most pagan of cultures, if they seek him out.

The great dividing point

The question could be asked, "If people can come to know God without hearing the full gospel message, then what is the point of preaching the gospel or sending missionaries to do so?" The answer is found in the Apostle Paul's address to the Athenians, where he went on to declare of idolatry, "In the past God overlooked such ignorance, but now he commands all people everywhere to repent." (Acts 17:30) The "now" of this passage refers to now that Christ has come and the gospel has been preached by the apostles. Since such preaching ended the period of God overlooking the ignorance of idolatry, those who heard the message of salvation through Christ were therefore responsible to respond to and embrace it. The true test that a person is seeking God is in how they reply when they hear the gospel of Christ. Jesus is the exact image of God (Hebrews 1:3) and those who reject Christ are rejecting God.

The gospel is the great dividing point—for after a person hears it, he is now in possession of the highest and fullest revelation of God needed for salvation. As Luke 12:48 says, "From everyone who has been given much, much will be demanded; and from the one who has been entrusted with much, much more will be asked." Jesus addresses this clearly in John 12:46-48. "I have come into the world as a light, so that no one who believes in me should stay in darkness. As for the person who hears my words but does not keep them, I do not judge him. For I did not come to judge the world, but to save it. There is a judge for the one who rejects me and does not accept my words; that very word which I spoke will condemn him on the last day." In other words, those who have heard the words of Jesus—the gospel—will be judged on the basis of what they have heard, so those who reject Christ after hearing his word will be condemned.

Jesus Christ was and is God incarnate, the supreme revelation of God to the human race. If a person hears the authentic message of the gospel or sees the life and witness of a faithful follower of Christ and still rejects Jesus, then it is proof that they are not seeking God. They are moving away from the light and not toward it. Of course, this is predicated on a faithful witness and a communication of the authentic gospel; a poor witness and a false representation of the gospel can certainly push people away from Christ and hinder the work of God in their lives.

Before the coming of Christ to Earth, the means by which God would save the world was somewhat hidden and for most people the knowledge of God came primarily through general revelation. But once Christ came, died, and rose again, the way of salvation became clear and unambiguous. The apostles were commanded to preach the gospel openly and to the ends of the Earth, and as a result it was proclaimed to the ancient world, beginning in Jerusalem, then into Judea, and then to the Gentile world. After more than 2,000 years, we are nearing the point where the gospel has been told worldwide.

In conclusion, God can judge those who have not heard the words of the gospel of Jesus audibly spoken to them on the basis of how they respond to the lesser revelations given to them. In fact, God will judge *all* people by how they respond to what he reveals to them. Each of us are given varying degrees of revelation, and we will all be judged accordingly. People will not be judged on whether or not they were terrified by any specific image or concept of judgment or hell. And God's final judgment will be on an individual basis, not according to the dominant or majority beliefs of the culture we belong to.

With this as the standard, how many people, then, will be saved: most or a few? Jesus appeared to answer this question in Luke 13:23-24. "Someone asked him 'Lord, are only a few people going to be saved?' He said to them, 'Make every effort to enter through the narrow door, because many, I tell you, will try to enter and will not be able to.'" He elaborated in Matthew 7:13-14. "Enter through the narrow gate. For wide is the gate and broad is the road that leads to destruction, and many enter through it. But small is the gate and narrow the road that leads to life, and only a few find it." The answer to the question lies between "many" and "few," which means we can safely conclude that most people will not be saved. The fact that we don't see hordes of people wanting to know about God, even in societies where the knowledge of God and the gospel is readily available, suggests that the majority of individuals simply do not want to know their Creator, regardless of their environment or culture. The desire to know God is a gift from him and inspired by God himself because none of us naturally seek him. "There is no one righteous, not even one; there is no one who understands, no one who seeks God." (Romans 3:10-11)

People also have varying thresholds for what it takes to believe in God. Even the apostles, who received the highest degree of revelation possible as witnesses of Christ's miracles, glory, and resurrection, had differing thresholds for belief. Thomas demanded physical proof that he could touch (John 20:24-29), while others believed solely on what was told to them (Matthew 8:8). The fact that God accommodates those of us who are "high threshold" people shows he is indeed a God of grace.

One final point: Jesus' parables of the bags of gold in Matthew 25:14-30 and the faithful and wise manager in Luke 12:47-48 make clear that much was expected of those who were entrusted with much, while less was expected of those entrusted with less. However, Jesus was not necessarily teaching that there are lesser punishments for those who know less. He was saying that more faith is expected from those who are given more revelation.

Although we cannot definitively answer Qiang's question of whether his father is in heaven, we do have more insight about how God will judge the human race and can say with categorical confidence that God does give an opportunity for *all* people to be saved. Because God is fair and just, we also know that he will judge fairly those who have never heard the full message of the gospel of Christ or Jesus' warnings about the final judgment. These truths are succinctly summarized in King David's discourse on God's judgment in Psalm 9:7-8, 10: "The Lord reigns forever; he has established his throne for judgment. He will judge the world in righteousness; he will govern the peoples with justice ... Those who know your name will trust in you, for you, Lord, have never forsaken those who seek you."

Chapter 5

Judgment by Fire

In my family growing up, my parents warned us kids in serious tones and in no uncertain terms that fire is not something to fool with. Perhaps we had seen what happened when other children played with it, or maybe had witnessed the careless use of it by adults. Either way, it frightened us to see desert brush fires or people who got badly burned. Still, if a fire was close enough, we would hop on our bikes and rush to the site. The smoke was the tell-tale sign that something was burning and in the process of being destroyed. All the warnings by the firefighters to stay away could not keep us from still watching the alarming scene from a distance.

I'll never forget when a home in our neighborhood burned down on Christmas Day. It seemed like a tragedy beyond compare that on such a happy day a family lost everything they owned in a matter of minutes. I don't recall hearing the sirens or seeing the smoke, but word of mouth spread quickly to us, and our entire family walked down the street and around the corner to see the charred walls and the scorched wooden beams. That was all that was left; it was consumed down to the foundation. This affected me greatly as a child; although my family didn't know the victims, I remember being very sad for them. From that day forward, no one had to impress upon me that fire was dangerous and something that should only be used in a controlled manner. Because of its destructive force, that home was gone forever.

Yet even that didn't quell my fascination with fire. I still attended trash fires, which until they were outlawed was one of the most common ways to get rid of things that could not be fixed, sold, or used and thus no longer had any value. Then there was the annual Christmas tree bonfire. Every year after the holiday was over, the trees were burned in one heaping pile at the local school yard on the same place where kids had recess when school was in session. This event, held right before sunset, drew a huge crowd, and no wonder. I never saw flames that big in my life—and while I was always excited before the trees were lit, that thrill quickly turned to a chilling fear that the giant flames might get out of control. I don't recall a fire truck being nearby; I guess the blaze always burned itself out. But I can still see the smoke, its massive, black pillar rising into the sky.

Of course, fire was just as fearful and common in the ancient world—and is mentioned countless times in the Bible. In many passages, fire refers to a physical blaze, but in other scriptural accounts, fire was meant to be understood metaphorically, representing a consuming punishment that ultimately destroyed an object, a group of people, or even a nation. The language of Psalm 21:9 is suggestive of this: "In his wrath the Lord will swallow them up, and his fire will consume them." The image of fire is used also to convey a purifying effect, especially for believers: "Everyone will be salted with fire." (Mark 9:49)

In a great number of biblical passages, fire is used to describe God's judgment upon sinful humanity. Whenever fire is used in the context of judgment, it conveys a destructive, consuming, final, and irreversible punishment. The following are only a few of the examples of this from the Old Testament:

- "The mighty man will become tinder and his work a spark; both will burn together, with no one to quench the fire." (Isaiah 1:31)
- "Let the fire reserved for your enemies consume them." (Isaiah 26:11)
- "Surely the day is coming; it will burn like a furnace. All the arrogant and every evildoer will be stubble, and that day that is coming will set them on fire." (Malachi 4:1)

God's all-consuming fire

In the New Testament the Greek word *pyr* is used when speaking of God's judgment by fire, and from Matthew to Revelation and many places in between, imagery of an all-consuming fire is used. In Deuteronomy 4:24, the Lord himself is described as "a consuming fire, a jealous God," and this idea is fully supported in the New Testament's passages on judgment.

The image of fire is also used for the fate of the wicked in the final punishment. Matthew 3:12 declares, "His winnowing fork is in his hand, and he will clear his threshing floor, gathering his wheat into the barn and burning up the chaff with unquenchable fire." This message, spoken by John the Baptist here and again in Luke 3:17, is that God will punish the wicked using fire that cannot be put out. The term "unquenchable" means that the fire is inevitable and unstoppable; therefore, the punishment cannot be avoided or thwarted. The assumption is that the chaff does not survive; it is consumed.

Next, in his parable of the weeds, Jesus said in Matthew 13:30, "Let both grow together until the harvest. At that time I will tell the harvesters: First collect the weeds and tie them in bundles to be burned." In his explanation of the parable in verses 37-39, Christ added that the angels themselves will throw all who do evil into the "fiery furnace." This phrase is used by Jesus several times and almost certainly refers to the lake of fire mentioned in the book of Revelation. In his parable of the net, Jesus said that at the end of the age "the angels will come and separate the wicked from the righteous and throw them into the fiery furnace, where there will be weeping and gnashing of teeth." (Matthew 13:49-50) This ties to the harrowing words of Matthew 25:41, where Jesus said of the king in his parable of the sheep and the goats, "Then he will say to those on his left, 'Depart from me, you who are cursed, into the eternal fire prepared for the devil and his angels.'"

Two other verses prior to Revelation are notable. Paul wrote of God's final assessment of Christians in 1 Corinthians 3:13, "His work will be shown for what it is, because the Day will bring it to light. It will be revealed with fire, and the fire will test the quality of each man's work." This refers to the burning up on the Day of Judgment of the believer's work that was not based on a solid foundation. Even more, Hebrews 10:26-27 states, "If we deliberately keep on sinning after we have received the knowledge of the truth, no sacrifice for sins is left, but only a fearful expectation of judgment and of raging fire that will consume the enemies of God." This passage warns that rejecting the sacrifice that Christ made for our sins will result in a terrible punishment of consuming fire at the final judgment. The writer of Hebrews then adds a consolation for his readers. "But we are not of those who shrink back and are destroyed, but of those who believe and are saved."

Speaking of the beast and the false prophet, Revelation 19:20 reveals that "the two of them were thrown alive into the fiery lake of burning sulfur." Bible scholars speculate the beast refers to the Antichrist, while the false prophet is a lieutenant of the Antichrist who possesses supernatural abilities. Whoever they really are, their fate is clear. Meanwhile, Revelation 20:10 states that "the devil, who deceived them, was thrown into the lake of burning sulfur where the beast and the false prophet had been thrown. They will be tormented day and night for ever and ever." Revelation 20:14-15 adds, "The lake of fire is the second death. If anyone's name was not found written in the book of life, he was thrown into the lake of fire."

Several of the passages already cited in this chapter (Malachi 4:1, Matthew 13:30, Matthew 25:41, and all four verses from Revelation) are a direct reference to fire as God's final judgment on the wicked at the end of time—not to a judgment that occurs on Earth or in this life. Likewise, the other parables from Matthew describe the same punishment of the wicked at the final judgment. It is not an earthly or temporary judgment.

These scriptures strongly assert that God's punishment of the wicked on the great Day of Judgment will be complete, permanent, and irreversible. It will not be a controlled burn that only singes or chars or attempts to achieve restoration, nor will it be a punishment for the purpose of tormenting; it will fully consume and destroy.

Cosmic destruction

It's easy to forget that the visible universe God created consists primarily of elements on fire. Our own sun is a raging ball of fire with a surface temperature of 10,000 degrees Fahrenheit and flames that shoot out into space for hundreds of miles. It is only one of billions of stars in the Milky Way Galaxy, each one a giant atomic furnace emanating heat and light in all directions, and our galaxy is just one of the billions of others in the universe.

Of course, we prefer not to look at what God destroys. It brings sadness or fear, while what he creates fosters joy and hope. This is understandable, for God's creation is awe-inspiring and brings us pleasure and wonder when we see ourselves in the context of what he has majestically made (Psalm 8:3-4). We know God created the stars and many of us love to gaze at them, but unless we have knowledge of astronomy, we seldom consider the fact that some of the stars we see are actually in the process of being destroyed. Scientists have learned that stars have a lifespan, and when their nuclear energy is used up, they collapse and then explode cataclysmically, creating a supernova. This is when most of the star's mass is ejected in the explosion and thrown out into space, resulting in a brilliant display of hot gases and dust called a nebula. The beautiful Crab Nebula is the result of a supernova explosion that occurred in our Milky Way Galaxy in 1054 A.D. These explosions are exceedingly bright and although they last only a few months, they outshine even the galaxies they reside in. Chinese astronomers observed supernovae explosions as long ago as 185 A.D. Although supernovae occur rarely in a typical galaxy, because there are billions of galaxies, stars are being destroyed constantly in the universe, a cycle of destruction that has been occurring since they were first created.

Yet the cosmic annihilation doesn't stop there. After a supernova explosion, the collapsed star will usually form a neutron star consisting of compacted neutrons. In the neutron star, the basic structure of the atom is destroyed. If the collapsing star has enough mass, the matter can fall in to the point that even the neutrons are compacted into one extremely dense mass. This forms a black hole, which creates a gravitational field so strong that it allows nothing in its vicinity to escape, pulling in everything around it, including light. In this environment, even matter as we know it is eliminated!

How does this apply to the topic of judgment? Because this is undeniable proof that God is indeed able to wholly destroy *anything* that he creates, even to where it is as though it never existed. With such power at his command, there seems to be no limit to what God says he can destroy. In both the Old and New Testaments, we find many passages that describe events involving the destruction of living things, people, towns, nations, and even of the heavens. Certainly, if God can create, he also has the right to destroy anything that he creates, even things that he initially created for a much higher, albeit temporary purpose. Psalm 10:16 is unwavering in its declaration, "The Lord is King for ever and ever; the nations will perish from his land." After the Israelites abandoned the Lord and worshipped the golden calf they fabricated, God threatened to destroy them entirely (Exodus 32). It was only after Moses pleaded with him to spare the people that God relented.

It is logical, then, that if a created thing has a beginning, then it will probably have an ending. Ecclesiastes 3:1-3 affirms, "There is a time for everything, and a season for every activity under heaven: a time to be born and a time to die, a time to plant and a time to uproot, a time to kill and a time to heal, a time to tear down and a time to build." The Apostle Peter proclaimed, "But the day of the Lord will come like a thief. The heavens will disappear with a roar; the elements will be destroyed by fire, and the earth and everything in it will be laid bare. Since everything will be destroyed in this way, what kind of people ought you to be? You ought to live holy and godly lives as you look forward to the day of God and speed its coming. That day will bring about the destruction of the heavens by fire, and the elements will melt in the heat." (2 Peter 3:10-12) Peter was no astronomer, but he did understand the power of God to create and to destroy! If God can (and will) destroy even the heavens, then he can certainly destroy us if we ignore his commands and reject his plan for our lives.

Two words, several views of destruction

In the New Testament, the two Greek words used for "destroy" in the context of judgment are *apollumi* and *olethros.* The first, *apollumi,* is mostly translated in English Bibles as either "perish" or "destroy." It is unclear, then, why the translators select perish in some cases, though the choice could reflect the theological bias of the translator since perish has a softer implication than destroy.

Apollumi appears in Matthew 10:28, where Jesus declares, "Do not be afraid of those that kill the body but cannot kill the soul. Rather, be afraid of the One who can destroy both soul and body in hell." This is the most unambiguous statement in the Bible about the nature of the final punishment of the wicked. It is not allegorical, symbolic, or a part of a parable. Jesus definitively states that the soul and body of those who are condemned by God are destroyed.

Apollumi can also mean "lost," as it is translated in the parables of the lost sheep, the lost coin, and the lost son (Luke 15). But as in all languages where there are multiple meanings of the same word, the meaning becomes obvious from the context of the discussion. For example, everyone knows the difference between "light" when referring to a light punishment, a light bulb, or to light a fire. The "lost" parables describe the process whereby God seeks and saves those who are lost spiritually and brings them to the safety of a relationship with him. A person who is lost spiritually is not necessarily lost forever, but can be found by God and saved. In contrast, a parable or passage describing the final punishment of the wicked will not use *apollumi* to mean "lost" since the context requires a meaning of perish or destroy. In these cases, the person is in the process of being punished by God, not saved. Although they were "lost" as humans on Earth, because they did not love the truth or repent, after death they will receive an eternal and irreversible punishment.

Another use of *apollumi* is "ruined," as in the ruined wineskins of Luke 5:37. Some commentators use these examples to argue that the wicked are not really destroyed at the final judgment, but instead experience only ruin, loss of well-being, and spiritual destitution. Some popular modern views use the term destruction in an allegorical sense to state that people exist forever in some dark and negative state, not a real, true, or final destruction. Of course, unbelievers do experience loss of well-being and spiritual destitution in this life. But the final punishment is much more than that. It is destruction by fire, and something that is thrown into a fire is not merely "ruined." The fire consumes it. So, while "ruined" and "destroyed" can mean virtually the same thing in the context of a wineskin, in that if a wineskin is ruined it cannot be used as a wineskin anymore, the parable of the wineskins is decidedly not about the final judgment.

Why is this discussion of meanings and context important? There are some Bible teachers who feel they can simply choose between multiple meanings of a Greek word to come up with an interpretation that best fits their theology or personal preference. But "shopping around" to find a meaning for a word apart from context is dishonest and is not rightly dividing the word of truth (2 Timothy 2:15). Because a word means one thing in one passage does not allow it to mean the same thing in other passages. *Apollumi* in the context of final punishment always means destroy or perish.

Notable references in the New Testament to the wicked perishing or being destroyed using the Greek word *apollumi* or a form of it include:

- "The one who hears my words and does not put them into practice is like a man who built a house on the ground without a foundation. The moment the torrent struck that house, it collapsed and its destruction was complete." (Luke 6:49)

- "For wide is the gate and broad is the road that leads to destruction." (Matthew 7:13) I can hardly imagine that Jesus was really saying, "Broad is the road that leads to a loss of well-being." It can only be referring to the final day of punishment for those who do not seek God and follow the narrow road.

- "But unless you repent, you too will all perish." (Luke 13:3) It is not likely that Jesus was declaring that those who were listening to him will be destroyed in a similar manner (to those that died by the falling tower in verse 4) if they don't repent. Rather, he was stating the fact that people will perish at the final punishment if they don't repent of their sins before God.

- "For God so loved the world that he gave his one and only Son, that whoever believes in him shall not perish but have eternal life." (John 3:16) This famous verse has been memorized by millions of people. Understood correctly, it not only declares that we are given salvation as a free gift through our faith in Christ and his finished work on the cross, but we will avert God's final punishment if we believe. Yet often overlooked is the fact that the converse is also true: those who refuse to believe after hearing the gospel will perish. Based on the use of *apollumi*, perish here can only mean eternal destruction that is irreversible. And Jesus gives no suggestion that those who don't believe could be saved through some other means *after* perishing.

Four more New Testament verses worth exploring here begin with Philippians 3:18-20. The Apostle Paul wrote about the "enemies of the cross of Christ" and stated, "Their destiny is destruction, their god is their stomach, and their glory is in their shame. Their mind is on earthly things. But our citizenship is in heaven." Paul contrasted the final destiny of the wicked (complete destruction) with the final destiny of those who are in Christ (heaven). Two passages that strongly imply there are only two paths for people at the final judgment, salvation or destruction, are Hebrews 10:39 ("We are not of those who shrink back and are destroyed, but of those who believe and are saved.") and James 4:12 ("There is only one Lawgiver and Judge, the one who is able to save and destroy.") If there are other paths that can be taken, they certainly would have been mentioned.

Finally, the Apostle Peter stated in 2 Peter 3:7, "By the same word the present heavens and earth are reserved for fire, being kept for the day of judgment and the destruction of ungodly men." It has been debated whether this passage is referring to the physical destruction of the ungodly at the coming of Christ or their destruction at the final judgment. It is likely the latter since many believe the present Earth will be destroyed at the time of the Day of Judgment and the commencement of the new heavens and Earth, not at the time of Christ's return to Earth. Other New Testament verses that use *apollumi* (or a form of it) to convey that the wicked will perish are Romans 2:12 and 9:22, 1 Corinthians 1:18, 2 Corinthians 2:15 and 4:3, Philippians 1:28, 2 Thessalonians 2:10, 2 Peter 2:3 and 3:9, Jude 11, and Revelation 17:8.

The Greek word *olethros* also means "destruction," especially in the sense of killing or slaying. *Olethros* is used in 1 Thessalonians 5:3 ("While people are saying, 'Peace and safety,' destruction will come upon them suddenly.") and 2 Thessalonians 1:9 ("They will be punished with everlasting destruction."). The combination of "everlasting" and "destruction" in the latter verse is curious, and some try to emphasize everlasting to argue that punishment in hell will go on forever. But a reading of the verse in its context does not allow this because it states that the punishment will be destruction that is final and therefore cannot be reversed, regardless of the meaning of "everlasting."

The final judgment and punishment will be a time of solemn sadness because, although the wicked were created for a higher purpose, they did not fulfill that purpose and forfeited the great opportunity and potential that could have been theirs. Just as a house that burns to the ground is gone forever, so it will be with the wicked. As we continue our discussion on final and ultimate punishment, let's look next at the word hell—and the various ways it is presented in Scripture.

Chapter 6

Hell in the New Testament

As a child, it scared me whenever my dad used the word "hell." While he usually said it when he made a mistake (like banging his finger when working on the engine of his 1958 Jaguar sports car), I really didn't know what he meant. But it was the tone of his voice that made it sound bad. It seemed that hell was a word only adults could say since they alone were the only ones who knew its meaning.

For a while, the use of hell as an expletive fell out of fashion, but it seems to be making a comeback. Political leaders have discovered that the command "go to hell" can be useful to raise the emotions of their opponents, much like politicians decades earlier used to accuse their foes of being like Hitler. In 2017, Vicente Fox, a previous president of Mexico, told newly-elected President of the United States Donald Trump to go to hell in response to his proposed border policies. A year later, Iran's ruling supreme leader, Ayatollah Sayyid Ali Hosseini Khamenei, also told President Trump, "You will go to hell with your failures," after Trump pulled out of the nuclear weapons agreement struck between Iran and former President Barack Obama. Khamenei was certain that Trump's decisions made him worthy of punishment in hell and wanted the world to know it.

Although most people have used the word hell, I suspect most have no idea what it really refers to. People usually reserve "go to hell" for their worst enemies. We may also use it in a fit of rage to express our own frustration at someone, even if we don't believe that individual is truly bad. However, "go to hell" is understood by all to be the absolute worst thing that we can possibly wish upon another person.

Not everyone believes there is such a place as hell. Most believe it is probably a place of unbearable punishment, but descriptions of it vary wildly. So what is it? *Where* is it, if it is a place at all? Is it accurately described in church teachings? What does the Bible actually say about it? The final and ultimate punishment that God will inflict on the wicked is referred to in the English translations of the New Testament as "hell." Unfortunately, there are three Greek words that are translated as hell in some of these translations—Hades, Tartarus, and Gehenna—and this has caused confusion for centuries.

Hell's origins

In actuality, hell was originally a medieval word fitted into the Christian idiom during the Middle Ages, long after the early period of the Christian church. The English word hell was derived from either the Old English word *hel*, referring to the place of the dead, or from Old Norse and Germanic words of the same root that suggested punishment in a hidden underworld thought to be in the depths of the Earth.

Since the Middle Ages, the concept of hell was influenced by popular beliefs such as hell being the place where bad people go after they die. I once saw an old man with long hair and a beard driving a beat-up pickup truck on the highway. The truck's bumper sticker read, "SPEED ON BRO, HELL

AIN'T HALF FULL YET!" Another popular idea is that hell is the home of Satan and the place where all his followers eventually go to live forever. It is a common joke among many that hell won't be so bad as long as they can see their friends there and be able to party with them.

In studying and applying the Bible, medieval teachers of the Middle Ages did not distinguish between the different Greek words for hell and used the Greek concepts of Hades and Tartarus as models for the biblical hell. This mindset carried over into the medieval church, some translations of the Bible, and has extended all the way to many present-day churches. The King James translation of the Bible does little to sort out the Greek words, and in some cases brings even more confusion to the subject. Some commentators believe that the word hell does not belong in the Bible at all, but is merely a holdover from Greek mythology and the Middle Ages.

It is unfortunate that the true meanings of the Greek words have been ignored for much of church history. Before the topic of hell can be breached, the origins and actual meanings of all three Greek words must be examined.

Hades

Hades was the Greek word for the place of the dead and was well used in ancient Greek culture. The word was taken from the name Hades, the god of the underworld and the ruler of the dead. The realm of Hades was revealed in detail in Greek mythology. It was a dark and gloomy place, the final resting place of all dead souls who were judged on their virtuous life or lack thereof. Hades was entered by crossing the River Styx. On the other side of the river, Hades was guarded by Cerberus, a vicious three-headed dog. In the forecourt of the palace of Hades sat three judges waiting to assess the dead as they arrived.

Hades the Greek god sat in his palace on a throne of bones, and was seen as a just but stern deity that was unmoved by prayer. He was not a judge, but rather the caretaker of the place of the dead and the one who executed punishment of the wicked. He went to great lengths to make sure no one who was being punished ever got out of Hades, except for unusual circumstances and only with his permission. Hades was held in awe and fear by the Greeks, who avoided even speaking his name.

Greek gods bore more resemblance to humanity than a sovereign Creator God, and many of their actions resembled some of the worst of human behavior. Killing their opponents and even their close relatives to maintain power or exact revenge was common. Zeus was the supreme deity of the Greek pantheon, being the king of the gods, who embodied aspects of the sky, weather, and law and order. As a child he was saved by his mother from being swallowed up by his father Kronos. Zeus later fought his father and was able to free his brothers and sisters from Kronos, who regurgitated them. Zeus drew lots with his brothers over the division of the cosmos and ended up being the ruler of the heavens. His wife was Hera, queen of the heavens, and by her he fathered a number of minor gods and goddesses. However, not being a moral god, Zeus was not faithful to his wife and had numerous affairs with other goddesses, nymphs, and even human women, producing by them other gods, heroes, and even monsters. Hera's anger over his misbehavior drove her to incite a full-scale rebellion of the gods against Zeus, with him ending up being tied up on a couch, later to be rescued by one of his guards.

Needless to say, the Greek gods and the mythology surrounding them did not provide much inspiration for the betterment of the human condition, and certainly did not reflect the high moral ideals of the Hebrew culture and religion.

Although the word Hades did not express any exclusively Christian concepts, it eventually came to be used in early Greek-speaking churches and in the New Testament to refer to the place for the dead, roughly equivalent to the Old Testament word *Sheol.* Some Bible teachers assert that the precise meaning of a Greek word will in all cases give a more accurate meaning of the New Testament passage using that word. However, it is clear the early Christian church did not accept the mythology of Hades but imposed a Christian meaning on the word. The biblical use of Hades does not necessarily imply eternal punishment, and certainly does not indicate any connection to Greek mythology.

The King James Version of the Bible translates Hades as "hell" in most New Testament passages. But if the word "Hades" and the words "lake of fire" in Revelation 20:14 were also translated as "hell" (which it is by most commentators' definition), then the verse would read: "Then death and *hell* will be thrown into *hell.*" Since this obviously doesn't make any sense, there must be something wrong with the English translation of Hades as hell. The New King James Version corrects this error and does not translate Hades as hell. The New International Version translates Hades as hell in just one passage (Luke 16:23). This error has even been repeated in some versions of the Apostle's Creed, in which Christ is said to have "descended into hell." To avoid this confusing and erroneous statement, many versions of the creed use the translation "descended to the dead" and one version omits the sentence altogether.

The first use of the word Hades in the Bible is in Matthew 16:18 where, after Peter had confessed Christ as the Son of God, Jesus told him: "And I tell you that you are Peter, and on this rock I will build my church, and the gates of Hades will not overcome it." Here, Christ declared that death and its power was going to be conquered through the work of Christians advancing the gospel, beginning with Peter himself. The idea was that believers in Jesus would invade Hades, the place of the dead, and Hades would not be able to resist the power of salvation presented to people through their preaching and testimony.

Luke 16:19-31 records the parable of Lazarus and the rich man. In it, Jesus describes a wealthy person who lived a selfish life, died, and then awaited his final judgment in Hades, the place of the dead. While he suffered in Hades he begged Abraham to go to his family members on Earth and warn them about the place so that they wouldn't have to go there. "In hell, where he was in torment, he looked up and saw Abraham far away, with Lazarus by his side. So he called to him, 'Father Abraham, have pity on me and send Lazarus to dip the tip of his finger in water and cool my tongue, because I am in agony in this fire.'" (Luke 16:23-24) This parable is used by many to argue for the unending, conscious torment of the unrighteous after the Day of Judgment. However, this parable could not possibly be a description of the final and eternal state of the wicked. That the rich man's family members are still alive proves there are still people living on the Earth at this time (clearly the present Earth and not the "new earth" described in Revelation 21). Therefore, the final judgment had not yet happened since at that time no one will be on Earth, but everyone will be appearing before God to give account of their lives. Others believe this parable is not describing a real place at all, and was only being used by Jesus to teach a spiritual lesson. In either case, the suffering depicted in this parable cannot be the final punishment of the wicked. An important point to remember is that this story is a parable, and it is risky to formulate doctrine from parables.

Revelation contains two other interesting uses of Hades. In one, Jesus stated that he has conquered death and has power and authority over death and the place of the dead. "I am the Living One; I was dead, and behold I am alive for ever and ever! And I hold the keys of death and Hades." (Revelation 1:18) The second use described events at the end of time. "The sea gave up the dead that were in it, and death and Hades gave up the dead that were in them, and each person was judged according to what he had done. Then death and Hades were thrown into the lake of fire." (Revelation 20:13-14) This passage clearly states that Hades, the place of the dead, and death itself will be destroyed forever. This is a great comfort and affirms the promise of Revelation 21:4 that all suffering, pain, and death will be done away with. There will be no separate place where they still exist. This also confirms the fact that Hades has nothing to do with the final destiny of the wicked, but can only be referring to some kind of temporary state that will ultimately be destroyed. Finally, in his second epistle, the Apostle Peter stated that "the Lord knows how to rescue godly men from trials and hold the unrighteous for the day of judgment," (2 Peter 2:9), meaning that God will somehow keep the wicked who have died separate and apart for the final judgment. This may suggest Hades as that temporary dwelling place.

In the end, while many people believe Hades is an accurate description of hell and use it when talking and teaching about hell, Hades must be an intermediate state for people awaiting final judgment, not the judgment itself, assuming it exists at all. If people use the word hell to refer to a *place* where the souls of the wicked are temporarily in torment, then what they are referring to is Hades. However, biblical references to Hades do not necessarily *prove* that such an intermediate state for the wicked as envisioned by many actually exists, since Scripture does not provide a complete and accurate description of it, even in the parable of the rich man, since this story is a parable that uses abundant metaphors.

Tartarus

The word Tartarus was also derived from Greek mythology. At first, Tartarus was a deity, but later came to be known as a region of the underworld, the lower level of Hades. It was reserved for the eternal punishment of wicked humans and evil gods, most notably the Titans, who were the second generation of gods within the Greek pantheon. Kronos, the ruling Titan, had imprisoned the Cyclops and three monsters in Tartarus. But Kronos' son Zeus released them from prison and used them to overthrow the Titans, many of whom were later thrown into Tartarus themselves. Tartarus was also inhabited by other ferocious monsters and depraved criminals. In the Theogony, a poem by Hesiod describing the origins and genealogies of the Greek gods, it was claimed that it took nine days for an anvil to fall from Earth to Tartarus. Within Tartarus was the "abyss," a bottomless pit from which anyone thrown into it could never escape.

In the New Testament, Tartarus refers to a place where wicked spirits or angels are sent to be punished or imprisoned temporarily. The main passage where Tartarus is used in the Bible (translated as hell) is 2 Peter 2:4, which states, "God did not spare angels when they sinned, but sent them to hell, putting them in gloomy dungeons to be held for judgment." In addition, Jude 6 states, "And the angels who did not keep their positions of authority but abandoned their own home—these he has kept in darkness, bound with everlasting chains for judgment on the great Day." This seems to refer to the Tartarus in the verse from 2 Peter. The context of both passages is a discussion of the condemnation and punishment of false teachers, suggesting that they, upon death, will be imprisoned for a time in Tartarus along with the fallen angels.

The term "abyss" in the New Testament could also refer to Tartarus because of the close association of this term with the Tartarus of Greek mythology. As Jesus cast out the demons who called themselves "Legion" from a man who lived in the region of the Gerasenes, the demons begged Christ to not command them to go into the abyss (Luke 8:31). Apparently, the demons knew full well what the abyss was and what it meant to be sent there. It was the place where God will temporarily incarcerate evil spiritual powers during the last days as described in Revelation 20:1-3. "And I saw an angel coming down out of heaven, having the key to the Abyss and holding in his hand a great chain. He seized the dragon, that ancient serpent, who is the devil, or Satan, and bound him for a thousand years. He threw him into the Abyss, and locked and sealed it over him."

Isaiah 24:21-22 also mentions a temporary holding place for evil spirits. "In that day the Lord will punish the powers in the heavens above and the kings on the earth below. They will be herded together like prisoners bound in a dungeon; they will be shut up in prison and be punished after many days." This Old Testament passage suggests a place similar to Tartarus of the New Testament.

Again, the early Christian church did not accept the Greek mythology of Tartarus and the abyss, but imposed Christian meanings on the words as being places of temporary incarceration for fallen angels, false teachers, and possibly even all of the wicked. But, like Hades, Tartarus was not the final destination of the wicked. Translating Tartarus as "hell" is confusing and hinders our understanding of the final judgment and punishment.

Gehenna

In the Old Testament, we discover that Jeremiah had a very difficult job, one none of us would want for any amount of money. He was to be a prophet to the nations, "to uproot and tear down, to destroy and overthrow, to build and to plant." (Jeremiah 1:10) Needless to say, he was not well-liked by the people; he had only a few friends which included his loyal scribe Baruch. He was imprisoned a number of times and once thrown into a deep muddy cistern for days for proclaiming God's coming judgment.

One of his vital assignments was to denounce those who had sacrificed their children to Baal, one of the Canaanite gods. God told Jeremiah, "The people of Judah have done evil in my eyes, declares the Lord. They have set up their detestable idols in the house that bears my Name and have defiled it. They have built the high places of Topheth in the Valley of Ben Hinnom to burn their sons and daughters in the fire—something I did not command, nor did it enter my mind." (Jeremiah 7:30-31) Ben Hinnom was located below just and to the southwest of ancient Jerusalem. Topheth was an Aramaic word meaning "fireplace" or "furnace" and came to signify a fire pit into which the children were thrown alive as a sacrifice. Several kings committed this sin years before the time of Jeremiah, including Ahaz (2 Kings 16:3) and Manasseh (2 Kings 21:6).

Curiously, God commanded Jeremiah to purchase a new pottery jar, then take the elders and priests with him and stand at the Potsherd Gate of Jerusalem overlooking the Valley of Ben Hinnom. The Potsherd Gate was the portal through which potters in that section of town discarded their broken and useless pots. Once there, Jeremiah denounced the kings of Judah and the people of Jerusalem. Announcing the words of the Lord, Jeremiah said, "Listen! I am going to bring a disaster on this place that will make the ears of everyone who hears of it tingle. For they have forsaken me and made this a place of foreign gods; they have burned sacrifices in it to gods that neither they nor their fathers nor the kings of Judah ever knew, and they have filled this place with the blood of the innocent. They have built the high places of Baal to burn their sons in the fire as offerings to Baal—something I did not command nor mention, nor did it enter my mind." He solemnly concluded: "So beware, the days are coming, declares the Lord, when people will no longer call this place Topheth or the Valley of Ben Hinnom, but the Valley of Slaughter." (Jeremiah 19:3-6)

God's promise was that the same place used to murder children was also going to be used by the Lord to slaughter those guilty of that grievous sin. Jeremiah then issued the decree that Jerusalem was to be taken by their enemies, the people in it killed, and their bodies left to become food for the carrion birds. In a vivid visual culmination of his declaration, Jeremiah smashed the new jar into pieces before the elders and priests and prophesied that God, in the same way, was going to shatter their city and nation. Just as the broken pot could not be repaired, this signified a final and irreversible judgment upon the wicked. The pieces of the broken pot were added to the countless sherds scattered on the ground outside the Potsherd Gate. This showed that God had in the past destroyed many other peoples and nations for similar reasons, and his warnings should not be taken lightly. For his obedience to God, Jeremiah was put into stocks.

As prophesied, Jerusalem came under siege in 589 B.C. by the Babylonians under Nebuchadnezzar. During this time, the inhabitants of the city endured horrible deprivation. The walls were breached, Jerusalem was destroyed, and thousands of Israelites were killed. Those that survived were taken into captivity. Those who were judged not strong enough to be of any use to the king were slaughtered, and they, along with the dead killed in battle, were disposed of in the Valley of Ben Hinnom. This valley eventually came to be known as "Ge Hinnom," Hebrew for Valley of Hinnom, and was later shortened to Gehenna. The valley is thought by many to have later been used for the burning of garbage during the time of Christ. It is this name, Gehenna, which is used by Jesus in his teachings to describe the place of final punishment of the wicked.

Gehenna is translated as "hell" in English Bibles and has no connection to Hades or Greek mythology. But translating both Hades and Gehenna as "hell" is also confusing and hinders our understanding of the final punishment, since the final punishment as described by Jesus is clearly that of Gehenna, and not Hades. In this book, I will use the word hell to refer to the consuming fire of Gehenna.

The first mention of Gehenna for hell in Scripture is found in Matthew 5:22, where Jesus says, in the context of talking about anger toward a brother, "But anyone who says, 'You fool!' will be in danger of the fire of hell." Later, when he taught on lust and adultery, Christ instructed, "If your right eye causes you to sin, gouge it out and throw it away. It is better for you to lose one part of your body than for your whole body to be thrown into hell." (Matthew 5:29) The obvious implication is that if your entire body is cast into hell, you perish.

Matthew 10:28 provides one of the clearest statements to the method of God's punishment of the wicked. "Do not be afraid of those who kill the body but cannot kill the soul. Rather, be afraid of the One who can destroy both soul and body in hell." There is no indication that Jesus meant this to be taken allegorically; rather, it is an unambiguous warning to avoid Gehenna at all costs. The passage describes hell as a punishment wherein God will completely destroy both body and soul. There is no reference to or even hint of torment, torture, or the prolonging of pain. It is interesting that the parallel passage in Luke 12:5 simply says, "Fear Him who, after the killing of the body, has power to throw you into hell." Taking both passages together, being thrown into hell is equated with the destruction of the whole person in the fire of Gehenna.

In Mark 9:47-48 (the parallel passage of Matthew 5:29), Jesus said, "It is better for you to enter the kingdom of God with one eye than to have two eyes and be thrown into hell, where 'their worm does not die and the fire is not quenched.'" The references to the worm and fire are from Isaiah 66:24: "And they will go out and look upon the dead bodies of those who rebelled against me; their worm will not die, nor will their fire be quenched, and they will be loathsome to all mankind." The passage from Isaiah is sometimes used to argue for the unending, conscious torment view of hell. However, the context is clear that those observing the results of the judgment of God on sinful humanity are looking not at living beings, but at dead bodies. The image is not one of living bodies writhing in pain while they are being burned or eaten by worms, but of corpses that are already dead and decomposing. Further support for this is found earlier in Isaiah 66:16, which states, "For with fire and with his sword the Lord will execute judgment upon all men, and many will be those slain by the Lord." The sword mentioned in this passage may be the fire itself, or it could indicate that God will somehow kill those that are condemned before the actual destruction takes place.

It is interesting that Jesus associates Gehenna with the prophecy in Isaiah 66, suggesting that the scene described by Isaiah was prophesying both the burning and decaying refuse in the Valley of Hinnom years later during the time of Jesus, as well as the consuming fire of Gehenna at the end of time. It is also notable that the Valley of Hinnom, which represents Gehenna as the place where the wicked will be punished, was located directly below ancient Jerusalem, while the hill of Calvary where Jesus was punished (for our salvation) was located nearby but somewhere above ancient Jerusalem. The proximity of the sites to each other and the contrasting imagery of destruction and salvation cannot be ignored as coincidence. Here the two paths, the wide road and the narrow road, are geographically displayed by God. How ironic, too, is it that the valley used by the wicked to sacrifice children to false gods by throwing them into the fire provides an image of the Gehenna that God will someday use to punish the wicked in an unquenchable fire.

It is been noted that John does not mention "hell" (Gehenna) in his gospel. Likewise, the Apostle Paul does not mention Gehenna in any of his writings. The question must then be asked: were the two first century apostles ignorant of the reality of a final punishment? This seems quite impossible. To John, however, those that believe the gospel enter into eternal life, while those who refuse to believe will perish. Although John's is an abridged description of the final punishment, his use of the term "perish" (*apollumi*) captured all that he wanted to convey about how God will punish the unbelieving. The Apostle Paul was schooled in the Old Testament Scriptures and it is certain that he was well familiar with the references to the wicked being destroyed (explained in the next chapter). In Paul's teaching, the death at the final punishment was permanent, final, and accomplished by destruction. Speaking of the enemies of the cross of Christ, Philippians 3:19 declares, "Their destiny is destruction, their god is their stomach, and their glory is in their shame." It is also important to note that although the terms "perish" and "death" can be interpreted various ways, if John or Paul had meant them to be interpreted as unending torment or spiritual loss, they would have stated so clearly.

Real or metaphorical?

If the fire of Gehenna is a literal blaze, it's clear nothing physical could survive it, and according to Jesus' statement in Matthew 5:28, no living soul could survive it either. Yet even if the fire is metaphorical, its intent and effect are the same: nothing is to live. The purpose of the fire is to destroy anything thrown into it. If it was meant to burn partially in a controlled fashion, it would've been clearly stated.

Those who believe in the eternal conscious torment of the wicked like to think of the fire of Gehenna as being symbolic because it allows for an unending punishment where living souls survive in some form and endure excruciating suffering forever. Jonathan Edwards, a Puritan preacher of the 1700s, declared in his sermon, "Sinners in the Hands of an Angry God," that "it would be dreadful to suffer this fierceness and wrath of Almighty God one moment; but you must suffer it to all eternity. There will be no end to this exquisite horrible misery. When you look forward, you shall see a long forever, a boundless duration before you, which will swallow up your thoughts, and amaze your soul; and you will absolutely despair of ever having any deliverance, any end, any mitigation, any rest at all."

But once you explain Gehenna in metaphorical terms, then other things must match up to the symbolism. For example, the soul must be dead as Scripture says, but it must also still survive in some form. Death then, also becomes metaphorical; the soul is "dead" only in a vague spiritual sense, but still lives on to suffer indefinitely in the figurative fire. Viewing all of the components of the final judgment and punishment metaphorically breaks down, therefore, at some point. After all, it also makes sense that the anguish and gnashing of teeth described in these scenes occur when the sentence is pronounced at the time of judgment, not as an ongoing punishment that goes on forever. Gnashing teeth into eternity would require an indestructible set of teeth or some means of acquiring new teeth every few years or so. Such a thought is ridiculous. From this, we can conclude that the shame, humiliation, and anger experienced by the wicked at the final judgment will occur at the moment they are being judged before God, not as an intrinsic part of the punishment afterward.

Finally, consider this. If the wicked are conscious as they are punished into eternity, then Gehenna must be, in some sense, bearable, at least enough to survive it. If that's the case, then it cannot possibly be as bad as Jesus describes in the gospels. But we can't have it both ways, and Isaiah's added description of the ungodly seems to support that view. "The sinners in Zion are terrified; trembling grips the godless: 'Who of us can dwell with the consuming fire? Who of us can dwell with everlasting burning?'" (Isaiah 33:14) The answer? No one can survive a consuming fire.

In truth, Gehenna is to be a place that is unbearable, not habitable, and that results in *total* loss. Jesus spent a lot of time warning us about how complete and absolute the punishment will really be. The purpose of Gehenna is not to inflict pain indefinitely. To punish someone by continually or repeatedly burning them is unnecessary. Only a sadist takes pleasure in inflicting pain, and in the Bible God himself states a number of times that he takes no pleasure in the death of the wicked or in the punishment of people for their sins. He would much rather people repent of their wrongdoing and live happy, fruitful lives under his care. If there is even a possibility that a person can be saved, then the punishment will be short and temporary for the purpose of redemption. But when redemption is no longer possible, God has every right to completely end the person's life, both body and soul.

This leaves many people to conclude, "Is it not cruel, then, for God to destroy people?" In actuality, it is cruel for God to *not* destroy those who persist in their rebellious state. What is the Lord to do with those who have no love for him, have no place for him in their lives, and refuse to conform to his will and plan? He cannot preserve them for some other purpose that is acceptable only to them, and he will not create some special universe where they can exist while remaining against him. Think again of the trash fires; the items thrown into them are obsolete, have no function, and are not saved for some future purpose. There is no need to preserve them since there is nothing left that is redeemable. I believe this is the reason Jesus used Isaiah 66:24 passage to describe the final punishment of Gehenna. It's a place where those that remain in rebellion to God and have no further usefulness to him are taken to be destroyed. Killing the wicked demonstrates the compassion of God, since by ending the person's life and existence, he thus ends their suffering.

So what does the Old Testament have to say about the final punishment, the fate of the wicked, and God's sovereign justice? Plenty—and we will begin with one of the oldest stories in all of the Bible.

Chapter 7

Final Punishment in the Old Testament

Most of us have heard about the story of Job, a righteous man who lived in the ancient land of Uz somewhere in the Syrian desert near Damascus. At one time, he was exceedingly rich and prosperous, but Satan claimed that the reason for this was that God put a "hedge" around Job to buffer him from suffering and evil in the world (Job 1:10). To disprove the devil's claim, the Lord allowed Satan to take all that Job had— his livestock, his children, and lastly his health. Job found himself sitting on the ground amongst the ashes mourning and nursing his sores. Job's three friends, Eliphaz, Bildad, and Zophar, arrived to console him, but they only ended up lecturing him, and Job responded by engaging in extended arguments with them. Although their intentions were good, Job's friends relied on simplistic reasoning to imply that his suffering was evidence that he must be guilty of sin. They were convinced that the righteous do not suffer and therefore Job deserved the hardship he was experiencing. They engaged in long, theological discourses to try to prove their position to a broken and suffering man.

At one point in the saga, Zophar argued that in this life the wicked will always get what they deserve. He told Job, "Surely you know how it has been from of old, ever since man was placed on the earth, that the mirth of the wicked is brief, the joy of the godless lasts but a moment … What he toiled for he must give back uneaten; he will not enjoy the profit from his trading … When he has filled his belly, God will vent his burning anger against him and rain down his blows upon him." (Job 20:4-5, 18, 23)

However, Job would have none of this. He had lived long enough to know that the wicked do *not* always get what they deserve in this life. "Why do the wicked live on, growing old and increasing in power? They see their children established around them, their offspring before their eyes. Their homes are safe and free from fear; the rod of God is not on them." (Job 21:7-9) Job continued, "They spend their years in prosperity and go down to the grave in peace. Yet they say to God, 'Leave us alone! We have no desire to know your ways. Who is the Almighty, that we should serve him? What would we gain by praying to him?'" (Job 21:13-15) Job was not going to be fooled by simplistic explanations of how the wicked were always punished in this life while the righteous were always blessed. He knew by experience that simply was not true. He had seen many examples of powerful ungodly people who cared nothing for God nor for the needs and rights of other people. Job understood how the wicked seemed to enjoy life and avoid suffering, and how their power and riches appeared to protect them from calamity.

The best Job could do to explain the injustice was to say that all people—rich and poor, weak and strong—went to the same place when they died. "Can anyone teach knowledge to

God, since he judges even the highest? One man dies in full vigor, completely secure and at ease, his body well-nourished, his bones rich with marrow. Another man dies in bitterness of soul, never having enjoyed anything good. Side by side they lie in the dust, and worms cover them both." (Job 21:22-26) Though he knew that the wicked sometimes prospered, Job also discerned that eventually everyone faces the same fate: the grave. But this didn't fully answer the question of injustice, and there are only a few faint references to a final judgment in the book of Job. "For what is a man's lot from God above, his heritage from the Almighty on high? Is it not ruin for the wicked, disaster for those who do wrong?" (Job 31:2-3) Job knew that there must be a final accounting, even if he didn't fully understand it.

The writer of Psalm 10 also expressed his anguish over his belief that the wicked are not called to account in this life. He wrote regarding their view of God, "In his pride the wicked does not seek him; in all his thoughts there is no room for God. His ways are always prosperous; he is haughty and your laws are far from him ... Why does the wicked man revile God? Why does he say to himself, 'He won't call me to account?'" (Psalm 10:4-5, 13) It is an indisputable fact that many criminals continue to commit crimes because they to go unpunished, successful in escaping a day of accounting before the law. There are also those who revile and taunt God himself by flagrantly and knowingly rebelling against his commands. The Psalmist asks the obvious question: "If there is a God, where is he—and will he ever hold them responsible for their actions?"

If the Day of Judgment and the final punishment of the unrighteous are imminent, then they are very important topics that surely must be mentioned throughout the Bible, in both the Old and New Testaments. But *where* are the clear references to the final punishment in the Old Testament?

Sheol is the Hebrew word for the grave and is used consistently in the Old Testament to refer to the place of the dead. This is distinguished from the word *qeber*, which refers to the burial place. Sheol is also sometimes used poetically to describe the physical punishment of the wicked or the common lot of all fallen humanity. But Sheol, similar to the New Testament word Hades, does not have the connotation of being the place of God's final, eternal punishment of the wicked.

Sheol is improperly translated as "hell" in 31 key Old Testament passages in the King James Bible, but in other passages Sheol is correctly translated as "grave." This discrepancy has introduced much confusion into the study and understanding of the final punishment. Those that swear by the King James Bible sometimes cite these passages as proof of their concept of hell. However, newer translations of the Bible have eliminated these errors—and since these properly translated scriptures do not use the word hell, many conclude that the final destiny of the wicked is not addressed at all in the Old Testament. They say the concept and true nature of hell was only revealed later by Jesus.

However, this claim is based on a faulty view of the final punishment. In reality, there are many references to the final fate of the unrighteous in the Old Testament. Even more, they teach the same view of the final judgment as that found in the New Testament: that God will ultimately destroy the ungodly and the wicked.

Agreement of the Scriptures

We have already seen how Isaiah 66 and Jeremiah 7 and 19 foreshadowed the final judgment of the wicked. Elsewhere, some Old Testament passages link the term destruction to the grave (in reference to the physical destruction of the body). For example, Psalm 18:4-5 says, "The cords of death entangled me; the torrents of destruction overwhelmed me. The cords of the grave coiled around me; the snares of death confronted me." There are many Hebrew words translated as destruction in the Old Testament, with the word *bathah* being one of the more common. *Abaddon* is used occasionally to denote the physical destruction of the body that occurs in the grave. The Hebrew verb *abad* is used frequently in the Old Testament, and is translated as, "to perish" or "be destroyed," in many cases describing the process of being put to death. A close look at several Old Testament references show that where God himself is the one executing "destruction" toward humans, it is usually an irreversible punishment.

One of the main themes of Psalm 37 is that this life is not what it seems. While the wicked may appear to prosper, God will cut them off (v.9), they will perish (*abad*) and vanish (v.20), they will pass away and be no more (v.36), and they will all be destroyed (v. 38). The psalmist does not say how this will happen, but it is assumed that God is the one who executes this irreversible punishment. The statement in verse 39 that "all sinners will be destroyed" has the definite ring of final judgment.

There are several other prominent Old Testament passages that declare the wicked will ultimately perish or be destroyed:

- "Kiss the Son, lest he be angry and you be destroyed in your way, for his wrath can flare up in a moment. Blessed are all who take refuge in him." (Psalm 2:12) This passage refers to the future Messiah to whom all earthly kings, and all of humanity, will someday bow. Those who refuse to honor him will be destroyed.
- "Your hand will lay hold on all your enemies; your right hand will seize your foes. At the time of your appearing you will make them like a fiery furnace. In his wrath the Lord will swallow them up, and his fire will consume

them." (Psalm 21:8-9) God's enemies being destroyed in a fiery furnace echoes themes found in the parables of Jesus.

- "The senseless man does not know, fools do not understand, that though the wicked spring up like grass and all evildoers flourish, they will be forever destroyed. But you, O Lord, are exalted forever. For surely your enemies, O Lord, surely your enemies will perish; all evildoers will be scattered." (Psalm 92:6-9) To be "forever destroyed" is an eternal punishment that cannot be reversed.
- "The Lord watches over all who love him, but all the wicked he will destroy." (Psalm 145:20)
- "Zion will be redeemed with justice, her penitent ones with righteousness. But rebels and sinners will both be broken, and those who forsake the Lord will perish." (Isaiah 1:27-28)

Speaking of those who condemn the innocent to death, Psalm 94:23 states of God, "He will repay them for their sins and destroy them for their wickedness; the Lord our God will destroy them." In addition, Psalm 119:119 says of the Lord, "All the wicked of the earth you discard like dross." This speaks of the throwing away of the wicked, similar to that of destruction.

Proverbs, a book that deals almost exclusively with wisdom and how it is applied in this life, often describes the consequences of our actions, either positive or negative. A good example is found in Proverbs 5:22. "The evil deeds of a wicked man ensnare him; the cords of his sin hold him fast. He will die for lack of discipline, led astray by his own great folly."

But Proverbs also speaks to the destruction of the wicked that goes beyond natural consequences in this life:

- "A scoundrel and villain ... he will suddenly be destroyed—without remedy." (Proverbs 6:12, 15)

- "A false witness will perish, and whoever listens to him will be destroyed forever." (Proverbs 21:28)
- "A man who remains stiff-necked after many rebukes will suddenly be destroyed—without remedy." (Proverbs 29:1)

In many cases, the wicked do receive their punishment in this life through the outcomes of their foolish decisions. The rule of cause and effect is true. However, it is also a fact that people do not get punished for every sinful thing they do. Sadly, *most* sins go unpunished on this Earth; there is no justice or recourse for millions of people who have been wronged, oppressed, and even murdered.

An honest review of all of these passages forces us to face this fact: If the destruction described was only to be limited to a physical destruction on Earth, then as Job concluded it seems that these promises remain mostly unfulfilled. If it is argued that these passages mean that the wicked will be destroyed solely through physical death, it is not a convincing explanation since *all* people die. In that regard, there is no difference between the wicked and the righteous.

Asaph's complaint

Asaph was a godly man in the Bible who anguished over these problems, but eventually found answers after he heard the voice of God. A Levite that served in the temple, Asaph was trustworthy and answered directly to King David. He was one of three individuals commissioned by David to sing in the temple: Heman was the main musician, Asaph was his right-hand man, and Jeduthun joined them. The trio was set apart along with their sons to prophesy and play music to praise the Lord (1 Chronicles 25:1-2). Asaph played prominent roles when the Ark of the Covenant was taken to Jerusalem (1 Chronicles 15:16-19) and at the dedication of

Solomon's temple (2 Chronicles 5:12). Asaph was also a poet and songwriter with a dozen Psalms ascribed to him. Even three hundred years later, King Hezekiah used Asaph's songs of praise in the rededication of the temple and the people to the Lord (2 Chronicles 29:30). Asaph was certainly someone any Christian church pastor today would love to have on staff.

Psalm 73 was one of Asaph's most prominent Psalms. In it, he complained to God about how the wicked seemed to have the upper hand in everything they did. They were callous, prideful, and arrogant, yet they still had success in their evil endeavors. They were carefree, and increased in wealth even to the point of excess. There was even a time, Asaph revealed, when he envied them for their free-wheeling lifestyle. Perhaps he was tempted to think he would've been much better off joining these worldly men rather than serving God.

But then he realized that it was all an illusion; the success of the wicked from God's view was temporary. "When I tried to understand all this, it was oppressive to me till I entered the sanctuary of God; then I understood their final destiny. Surely you place them on slippery ground; you cast them down to ruin. How suddenly they are destroyed, completely swept away by terrors! As a dream when one awakes, so when you arise, O Lord, you will despise them as fantasies." (Psalm 73:16-20) Asaph realized that God was going to bring them to justice one day and that for them it will be complete destruction. "Those who are far from you will perish; you destroy all who are unfaithful to you. But as for me, it is good to be near God. I have made the Sovereign Lord my refuge; I will tell of all your deeds." (Psalm 73:27-28)

The "final destiny" of anyone is their eternal state, not a temporary one. Psalm 73 says the final destiny of the wicked is destruction; they will perish (*abad*), and it is God who will destroy them. This Psalm agrees well with Paul's statement in

Philippians 3:18-19 concerning the "enemies of the cross" whose "destiny is destruction." The psalmist is not referring to the results of natural consequences or even to the destruction of the body in the grave, but an actual judgment of God on the final day. Psalm 73 goes on to describe the final destiny of the righteous, which is salvation and a dwelling place with God in heaven, consistent with God's promises given to New Testament believers. Even more, most people instinctively understand that a final judgment will bring about real and permanent justice for those who have been wronged, persecuted, and unjustly convicted and imprisoned, as well as for those who are victims of the gross and flagrant disregard of God's commands to treat others with love and respect. Psalm 73 captures God's ultimate purpose in bringing all people to justice on judgment day.

While it is true that many Old Testament believers had an incomplete view of the final judgment and punishment, and some may have mixed together the concepts of temporal judgment with the final judgment, the overwhelming evidence is that the Old Testament describes the final state of the wicked as permanent, irrevocable destruction. It is clear that the Old Testament view of the final punishment is in agreement with the New Testament view: that both body and soul will perish.

Chapter 8

Objections to Destruction as Final Punishment

Earlier, we established that the punishment for the wicked after the final judgment will be destruction, not the traditional view of eternal conscious torment of the wicked, a term first cited in a previous chapter to refer to unending suffering that goes on and on forever. When I first undertook this study on the final judgment and punishment I focused solely on a personal study of Scripture. At one point a co-worker at the international student fellowship knew that I was researching these topics and suggested that I read a work by John Stott,[1] who happened to be my favorite author. I was amazed that I had never heard of it before. It was an obscure work that was not widely circulated, as in it, Stott expressed his views on a number of subjects, some of which contradicted the traditional views about hell and the nature of the final punishment.

His conclusions were very much the same as what I found from my personal studies. As my studies continued, I was

------

1 John R.W. Stott, *Evangelical Essentials: A Liberal-Evangelical Dialogue,* Questions from David Edwards, Intervarsity Press, 1989.

introduced to other authors that came to the same conclusions and provided additional confirmation including Edward Fudge and John Wenham.

Stott received much criticism from some of his contemporary colleagues for parting ways with traditional views. Proponents of those views cite a number of Bible passages that seem to contradict destruction as the final punishment. They also cite Scriptural terms such as "unquenchable fire," "undying worms," "gnashing of teeth," "smoke ascending forever," and "no rest day or night." Edward Fudge[2] demonstrates how these terms have no connection to the concept of unending conscious torment, despite the fact that traditionalists have imputed their own meaning on these terms, without proper Biblical support, throughout the years. We will look at these terms in more detail, as they will be mentioned again as the book unfolds.

Let's now look at some of the common objections to destruction as the final punishment.

Objection #1: Eternal punishment

In Matthew 25:45-46, in reply to the wicked on judgment day, God will say, "I tell you the truth, whatever you did not do for the least of these, you did not do for me. Then they will go away to eternal punishment, but the righteous to eternal life." This verse is used frequently to support eternal conscious torment. Others have used this passage to justify the idea of torture of the wicked in hell, where punishment is meted out in a dungeon-like setting forever without ceasing, similar to the punishment of the gods in the Hades of Greek mythology.

However, the term "eternal" does not necessarily mean that the punishment, and thus the pain and suffering, goes

---

2   E.W. Fudge, *The Fire That Consumes*, Verdict Publications, 1982.

on forever. In light of the many Bible verses referring to the destruction of the wicked, the logical meaning of eternal in this passage is that the punishment is final and irreversible, with no hope of ever going back to the previous state. After all, destruction is also eternal: it is final, irreversible, and its effects are permanent. In fact, the outcome of destruction is clearly more eternal than a punishment of continual suffering. Those who are in existence in a negative state can theoretically still be brought back to a positive state, but those who have been destroyed are destroyed forever. Punishment from God that results in pain and suffering that never ends is not obvious from the Matthew 25 passage.

The Greek word for "eternal" in the New Testament is *aionios,* and it is used in different contexts such as "eternal judgment," "eternal redemption," "eternal salvation," "eternal destruction," and "eternal punishment." Fudge[3] offers an excellent discussion of *aionios,* how these terms all refer to an action of God that happened or will happen *once,* but the results of which are eternal; the judgment, the redemption, the salvation, the destruction, and the punishment were or will be caused by a decisive action of God in time, but in each case the results were or will continue forever. So, "eternal punishment" means that God will in one act decisively punish the wicked with destruction, and its result is final and permanent.

Objection #2: Revelation 14

The judgment in Revelation 14 is also frequently used to support the idea of eternal conscious torment of the wicked. It begins, "If anyone worships the beast and his image and receives his mark on the forehead or on the hand, he, too, will drink of the wine of God's fury, which has been poured

---

3   Ibid.

full strength into the cup of his wrath. He will be tormented with burning sulfur in the presence of the holy angels and of the Lamb. And the smoke of their torment rises forever and ever. There is no rest day or night for those who worship the beast and his image, or for anyone who receives the mark of his name." (Revelation 14:9-11) But there are a number of reasons to not jump to hasty conclusions about this passage. The book of Revelation presents a series of images and scenes that are not necessarily in chronological order, including the judgment scene in Revelation 14.

Some interpret this scene as occurring at the final judgment, so that the mention of the punishment of those that worship the beast is a parenthesis within the main discussion of the events of the end time, so it could read, "By the way, those that worship the beast will also be punished with eternal fire at the final judgment." In this view, the statement in this passage serves as a guarantee that those that worship the beast will also be destroyed in the lake of fire at the final judgment along with all of the rest of the wicked, and the scene in Revelation 14 is the same as the "great white throne" judgment of Revelation 20.

But a thorough reading of Revelation suggests that these may be two separate events. Those punished in this passage are identified as those who worshipped the beast and received his mark during the great tribulation period, not unbelievers in general or all of the unrepentant throughout history. This scene may occur immediately after the great conflict on Earth described in Revelation 19:19-21 and the return of Christ to the Earth. That's when Jesus will vindicate and reward his followers for their faithful service during the great tribulation period, and the beast and those in rebellion to God are destroyed. After this conflict, the 1,000-year millennial reign of Christ and his followers begins. The final Day of Judgment where everyone else, believers and unbelievers, are judged occurs after that.

Revelation 14:9-11 also states that those who are being judged will be tormented before the holy angels and the Lamb (verse 10). This is different from the scene in Revelation 20, where all people will be brought before God to give an account of their lives, and those whose names were not found in the book of life are punished. Another evidence that the scene in Revelation 14 may not be the final Day of Judgment is the wording, "There is no rest day or night for those who worship the beast and his image." This implies that, at the time of this scene, day and night still exist. However, at the final judgment and afterward there will be no day or night since the glory of God and the lamp of the Lamb will provide the necessary light (Revelation 21:23). After the final judgment, no one will be living on the old Earth, for there will be a new heaven and Earth (Revelation 21:1). Fudge argues that the fire burning "day and night" does not mean that it will burn forever and ever, but that the fire will burn both during the day and the night, not stopping until it has completed its purpose.[4]

The language in Revelation 14:12-13 also suggests that this judgment event takes place when people are still living on the Earth and when (or immediately after) there is still conflict on the Earth. It reads, "This calls for patient endurance on the part of the saints who obey God's commandments and remain faithful to Jesus. Then I heard a voice from heaven say, 'Write: Blessed are the dead who die in the Lord from now on.'" Those that "die in the Lord from now on" must be in the midst of an earthly conflict that is still ongoing, not part of the final judgment event.

---

4   Ibid.

The use of the "lake of fire" occurs a number of times in Revelation at separate times. The following is a possible chronology of events in which God uses the "lake of fire" to punish his enemies:

1. The beast and the false prophet, immediately after the second coming of Christ and his victory over the beast, as recorded in Revelation 19:20.
2. Those that worship the beast and receive his mark, also after the coming of Christ, as recorded in Revelation 14:9-11. This may occur after the time when the armies of the beast are killed (Revelation 19:21).
3. Satan himself, after the last battle at the end of the millennial reign of Christ, recorded in Revelation 20:10.
4. Death and Hades, immediately preceding the final judgment (Revelation 20:14).
5. All those whose names were not written in the book of life at the final judgment (Revelation 20:14 and 21:8).

Next, some insist that Revelation 14:9-11 teaches the eternal conscious torment of the wicked in hell because "the smoke of their torment rises for ever and ever." However, smoke is not the same as fire; it is the result of fire. It is common knowledge that the only two things that remain after something is burned up are ashes and smoke. The image used in this passage is of smoke that remains after the fire has gone out.

The same language is used in Isaiah 34 to describe the destruction of Edom. "Edom's streams will be turned into pitch, her dust into burning sulfur; her land will become blazing pitch! It will not be quenched night and day; its smoke will rise forever." (Isaiah 34:9-10) Here, the fire will not be quenched day or night while it is burning and until it has accomplished its purpose. The fire eventually does go out because various animals eventually live in this land again (Isaiah 34:11-15).

Likewise, the fire used in Revelation 19:3 to destroy the city of Babylon results in smoke that "goes up forever and ever." The fire eventually goes out since the purpose of the fire will be to destroy a city, which contains only so much combustible material. It's the smoke that goes up forever that serves as proof that its destruction is complete. The image of ascending smoke is also found in Genesis 19:24-28 in the description of the destruction of the cities of Sodom and Gomorrah, and Jude confirms that this was an example of how God punishes the wicked by eternal fire (Jude 7). The fire was not eternal in time, but eternal in its effects, since these towns were destroyed forever, never to be rebuilt.

Therefore, language of smoke that rises forever does not indicate a fire that continues to burn forever, but that a severe and irreversible judgment of God has been executed. Most importantly, the image of smoke ascending forever in Revelation 14:9-13 was not meant to convey a lingering punishment of the wicked that went on without ceasing into eternity, and does not require that we accept the view that the wicked will suffer unending conscious torment in hell.

Finally, there are those who believe that fire that literally burns into eternity is necessary for the punishment of the devil as portrayed in Revelation 20:10. It says the devil will be thrown into the lake of fire to be "tormented day and night forever and ever," but there is still debate whether the devil will exist forever to endure this torment, or whether in the process of the torment he will be totally destroyed. The devil's soul is not indestructible as some maintain, and God can certainly destroy him if he chooses.

Objection #3: "Cease to exist"

For years, my wife and I have hosted weekly Bible studies in our home. One evening the topic of hell came up, and I revealed my belief that the wicked will not live forever in hell, but will instead be destroyed once and forever. A few people in attendance had not heard that before, and one jokingly exclaimed, "Well, they should really be happy about that!" The implication was that this was great news for the wicked because it was far more preferable to being tormented in hell for eternity. I was in full agreement that this *was* preferable, both for the wicked and for God who judges fairly. But since then a few acquaintances have expressed reservations against the idea of the final destruction of the wicked because, in their minds, it is not a real punishment just to have the wicked "cease to exist." It seemed unfair that they somehow got off lightly when justice demanded there should be a much greater punishment.

However, the idea that the wicked simply cease to exist is a mischaracterization of the destruction view of final punishment. This has arisen, in part, because of the teachings of the Jehovah's Witnesses that humans cease to exist upon physical death and their entrance into "the grave," which they equate with Hades of the New Testament. However, there is no suggestion in the Bible that the wicked simply "cease to exist" when they die physically. The Bible unreservedly states that all people must appear before God to give an account of their actions while on Earth on the Day of Judgment, and that this day will be a solemn and fearful event. There is nothing light about falling into the hands of the living God (Hebrews 10:31). For those who do not love God, his punishment involves a humiliating judgment, exclusion from the redeemed, and separation from God, culminating with final and total death by destruction.

We have no right to tell the Lord how much more or less severe he must punish others. We must accept the judgments and punishments God has chosen. As God spoke to Job,

"Will the one who contends with the Almighty correct him? Let him who accuses God answer him! ... Brace yourself like a man; I will question you, and you shall answer me. Would you discredit my justice? Would you condemn me to justify yourself?" (Job 40:2, 7-8)

Objection #4: Blackest darkness

A final objection to the destruction of the wicked as final punishment is the mention of "blackest darkness" in 2 Peter and Jude. In 2 Peter 2:17, the lives of false prophets and teachers are described, saying that blackest darkness is reserved for them. Jude 13 uses the same wording regarding the fate of false teachers. Critics ask, "Don't these two passages also describe hell? If so, then all of the images of fire and destruction must be metaphors, since darkness and destruction are both descriptions of hell that contradict each other if taken literally."

However, a deeper look at the two passages reveals they are specifically talking about false teachers and prophets, not humanity in general. Each reference to blackest darkness is preceded by metaphors describing the false teachers as: springs without water, clouds without rain, trees without fruit, wild waves of the sea, and a wandering star. Just as a shooting star appears to go off into the darkness forever, false prophets or teachers will be punished similarly. In context, therefore, blackest darkness is also a metaphor.

In 2 Peter 2:1-3, it is said of these prophets or teachers that "they will secretly introduce destructive heresies, even denying the sovereign Lord who bought them—bringing swift destruction upon themselves ... Their condemnation has long been hanging over them, and their destruction has not been sleeping." Peter states that the *ultimate* fate of these false teachers and prophets will be destruction, which is assumed to be at the final judgment.

With these four common objections refuted, the question can be asked of the final judgment, "What will that incredible day be like…and how should we view it as we anticipate its inevitable arrival?"

Chapter 9

The Augustine Contradiction

Born in 354 A.D. in present-day Algeria, Augustine was an early Christian theologian and philosopher whose writings greatly influenced the development of Christianity. Yet his early life was anything but saintly. His mother Monica was a committed Christian and prayed fervently for his conversion, but as a youth her son was said to have lived a hedonistic lifestyle. He associated with young men who boasted of their sexual exploits (it was during this period that he uttered his famous prayer, "Grant me chastity and continence, but not yet.") and at age 17 began an affair with a young woman in Carthage. By then, he had thrown off his mother's religion and gone to Carthage to study philosophy. There he became an adherent of the teachings of Mani, a Persian philosopher who taught a dualistic view of the world in which the forces of light and darkness are constantly at war with each other, but neither ever wins.

When Augustine later accepted a position teaching rhetoric in Milan, his mother disapproved but continued to pray for him. It was there that he attended the cathedral to hear the city's bishop, Ambrose, preach. Augustine was so impressed that he gave up Manicheism in favor of Neoplatonism, the philosophy of the Christians as well as the Roman pagans of that time.

After a long struggle with sexual sin detailed in his *Confessions*,[1] Augustine became a believer in Jesus Christ after reading Romans 13:13-14: "Let us behave decently, as in the daytime, not in orgies and drunkenness, not in sexual immorality or debauchery, not in dissension and jealousy. Rather, clothe yourselves with the Lord Jesus Christ, and do not think about how to gratify the desires of the sinful nature." After his conversion, Augustine wrote numerous books, founded a monastery, and became a priest at Hippo in Northern Africa and finally the bishop of Hippo. There he argued successfully against the Manicheans, and then the Donatists, who believed that priests must be sinless for valid sacraments to be given. He died in 430 A.D.

Augustine was a sincere believer powerfully converted from a sinful and decadent life, and his life and faith have inspired many to follow Christ through the centuries. He had much insight into the gospel, and his writings laid a theological framework that many other students of religion and believers in God have since followed. Augustine's quote, "You have made us for yourself, O Lord, and our hearts are restless until they rest in you," has inspired millions. However, Augustine was to some degree a product of his culture. He apparently never fully divorced himself from Manicheism, which is reflected in his dualistic theology. Plus, in adopting Neoplatonism, he embraced many Greek views of life and death that were popular at the time. Although his Christian faith was strong, Greek philosophy heavily influenced his theology.

---

1   Saint Augustine, *Confessions*, Henry Chadwick (Translator), Oxford University Press; 1 edition, 2009.

Augustine was in error on a number of issues, including some basic facts of science, the eternal virginity of Mary—and the final eternal state of the unbelieving. He advocated the use of state-supported violent force against those he considered heretics. He also believed in infant baptism to the point that he thought babies who died without being baptized were going to be condemned at the final judgment. Toward the end of his life, Augustine refined and retracted some of his earlier beliefs, but his view of the final judgment stood.

Fortunately, it is not necessary to adhere to everything that Augustine taught to receive the benefit of his more important teachings. But it *is* necessary to reject the errors that he introduced into Christian doctrine and exclude them from our belief and practice; for example, his support for and elaboration on the idea of the eternal conscious physical and mental torment of the wicked in hell. His writings found in *The City of God*[2] popularized this idea more than the works of any other theologian. It formed the basis for this theology into the Middle Ages for the Roman Catholic Church and also into the Reformation for most Protestant churches. Augustine's position has more recently been termed the "traditionalist" view, since it was historically the belief of all Catholic theologians and most of the Reformers, and is the current view of most Christian churches today.

What was Augustine's argument? He believed that, because God is so great and infinite, then any sin against God must also be equally as great and must be punished by an infinite punishment. In other words, if God is eternal, then his punishment against sin must also be eternal. This was a major justification for the belief in eternal conscious torment of unbelievers in hell, since by "eternal" he meant continuing on forever in time: a perpetual process of dying some call "eternal

---

2   Saint Augustine, *City of God*, Image, Abridged edition. 1958.

death." According to Anglican clergyman and theologian Philip Hughes,[3] Augustine's belief in eternal death forced him to literally redefine death to essentially mean being kept alive to suffer physical and emotional punishment, but without the power of actually dying.

This, of course, is an essential contradiction—but it's one that has been maintained by numerous theologians for centuries. To maintain this belief, Augustine developed elaborate theories on how God keeps people alive in hell by a special miraculous process so that they can be repeatedly tormented. God tortures people to near death, he postulated, only to revive them again so he can torment them again, a wretched process repeated over and over forever.

The dualistic nature of Augustine's theology extended past the final judgment. He maintained there will actually be two kingdoms after judgment day: one ruled by Christ and the other ruled by the devil, a view perhaps influenced by Manicheism. The righteous will enjoy God in heaven for eternity while the wicked will suffer in hell forever under the devil's power and rule. This was necessary since, in Augustine's mind, the wicked never really die but live on unhappily ever after with Satan and his angels.

Erroneous conclusions

Augustine's arguments are based on what I call "chain link" theology. It usually starts with a true idea from Scripture, the first link in the chain. It then builds a theology on a series of connecting chain links based on argument, logic, and extrapolation. "If this is true, then this other must be true, and then this must also be true." Thus, a chain of assertions is formed beginning with a true statement and ending with a conclusion that is not found in Scripture or true at all. Augustine's first

---

3   Philip Hughes, *The True Image*, Wm. B. Eerdmans Publishing Company. 1989.

statement that God is great, infinite, and eternal is obviously true. However, it's with the second and third links in the chain where his theology fails.

First, the assertion that sin against God is eternal is an odd statement and has no basis in Scripture. If it is infinite, in what sense? It is true that the sin of rebellion against God has eternal consequences *for us* if we never repent. But humans are finite sinful beings that are capable of only doing so much damage, and our sin against God, however rebellious it may be, does not really amount to much *against God*, certainly in the eternal sense. How is it possible for a finite creature to harm an infinite God infinitely? It makes no sense at all. Our lives are just a mist before God (James 4:14). Therefore, our sin doesn't affect anything—except in the sense that *we* remain separated from God and from each other. It does not affect the cosmos, God's eternal state, his authority, his power, or his intentions. God's plan will be accomplished regardless of the opposition, be it from humans or even evil spiritual powers. The fact that God can completely overcome and destroy his enemies is indisputable, and our rebellion against him, however disagreeable and saddening it is to him, does not threaten God or his sovereignty in any way.

Second, the statement that God's punishment of sin must also be eternal is equally erroneous. Since he is sovereign, God is not obligated to respond to our sin in any specific way. God does not have to obey laws; he makes them. And he certainly doesn't have to observe our rules of logic; he is the one from whom all wisdom, reason, and logic flow. Some might respond that since God is just and righteous, then he must punish sin. This is true, but it does not prove in any way *how* God must punish sin. He is free to execute whatever punishment he sees as fit, appropriate, and just.

In the end, Augustine's reasoning—that since God is so

great, any sin against him must be punished with an equally great punishment—is a gross misrepresentation of God's character as revealed throughout the Bible. Any human who punished their enemies in such a way would be rightly considered to be extremely arrogant and cruel. History is filled with such earthly rulers whose self-perceived greatness caused them to oppose their enemies with maximum brutality: Nero, Tamerlane, Stalin, Hitler, Mao Zedong, Edi Amin, and Pol Pot are just a few. Mongol emperor Genghis Khan, in his military campaigns to expand his kingdom, was said to come upon a city and demand total submission. Any who resisted were killed and their towns demolished. It is reported that he took great pleasure in slaughtering other humans. He even claimed to be doing this in obedience to Tengri, the Mongol Sky god, to punish the people for their sins. It is estimated that 30 million people died from 1211 to 1234 as a result of Khan's sadistic conquests.

To the tyrant and despot, cruel displays of power and extreme punishments somehow prove their own importance and greatness. But this was certainly not the attitude of Christ, our true ruler, who, although being the exact image of God and through whom the universe was created, gave up his greatness and power to become a common human being like us, and for our sake became our servant, suffering for us even to the point of death.

Chapter 10

Judgment Day Revealed

The Day of Judgment conjures up strong images in our minds. We generally think of it as an ominous event that produces fear, anxiety, and shame. From what we read in the Bible, it's an appointment all of us will have to keep, whether we want to or not. This will not be an opportunity for people to accuse those that they hated, address grievances, or get even. It will be for the sole purpose of each of us being judged individually before our Creator.

Most of the references in the Old and New Testaments to God punishing the wicked by fire and destroying them refer to the final punishment at the Day of Judgment. God's ultimate answer for injustice and sin is to bring the wicked to justice on that one ultimate day. Although the various writers of the Bible may have used different terms, they undoubtedly were referring to the same event—and, as we have seen, assuming that these terms refer to different events leads to complex and intricate theology not intended by the authors.

It is true that the term "day of the Lord" is used many times in the Old Testament for a day of reckoning or punishment by God, depending on the context. In some cases, it alludes to or refers directly to the final judgment. The term "the Day" as used by Paul in various passages in his epistles and in Hebrews 10:25, and the term "day of God" used in 2 Peter 3:12, sometimes suggest a broader event that includes the second coming of Christ. But these terms almost always include the final judgment. However, the "Day of Judgment" is used almost exclusively for the final judgment, especially in the New Testament teachings of Jesus from Matthew 10:15, 11:24, and 12:36.

The books of God

The story of Moses and the Israelites in the wilderness gives us insight into the final judgment. As they were travelling through the desert, Moses felt a tremendous responsibility for the people. He always saw them as one undivided nation chosen by God. At one point in their journey, the Israelites rejected God by making and worshipping the golden calf. Moses said to God, "Oh, what a great sin these people have committed! They have made themselves gods of gold. But now, please forgive their sin—but if not, then blot me out of the book you have written." (Exodus 32:31-32) Moses understood that God had a book containing a record of all those who were his people, who belonged to God's chosen nation, and who were to inherit his promises. Moses asked God to forgive the people for their rebellion so they could still inherit his blessings. But in his grief he despaired to the point that if God chose not to forgive, he wanted *everyone* to be removed from his blessing, including himself.

God reminded Moses that in his judgment he will separate the righteous from the wicked, even from within the people of Israel. He assured Moses, "Whoever has sinned against me I will blot out of my book." (Exodus 32:33) He promised that the Israelites who rejected the true God and deliberately sinned against him by worshipping the golden calf would be removed from his book. The names of those who stayed faithful to him would remain in his book and inherit the blessings promised to the people of Israel.

David's declaration to God in Psalm 9:5 reveals that God's record books include the names of *all* people: "You have rebuked the nations and destroyed the wicked; you have blotted out their name for ever and ever." The Lord indeed records the deeds of every human on Earth. David's prayer concerning the wicked in Psalm 69:28 is even more explicit: "May they be blotted out of the book of life and not be listed with the righteous." This Psalm described David's sufferings at the hands of his persecutors and also foreshadowed the sufferings of the future Messiah and the judgment of those who would reject the Messiah.

The most complete and non-allegorical description of the Day of Judgment is found in Revelation 20:11-15. "And I saw a great white throne and him who was seated on it. Earth and sky fled from his presence, and there was no place for them. And I saw the dead, great and small, standing before the throne, and books were opened. Another book was opened, which is the book of life. The dead were judged according to what they had done as recorded in the books. The sea gave up the dead that were in it, and death and Hades gave up the dead that were in them, and each person was judged according to what he had done. Then death and Hades were thrown into the lake of fire. The lake of fire is the second death. If anyone's name was not found written in the book of life, he was thrown into the lake of fire." The separation of the righteous from the wicked in this account strikingly parallels the separation of the sheep from the goats in Matthew 25:31-46. This account also parallels the story of God's judgment of the Israelites who worshipped the golden calf. The "books" mentioned in this passage are the record of the true actions of the lives of those who are being judged. The "book of life" is apparently a separate book and those whose names were found in it inherit the blessings of God and promise of eternal life. Those whose names are blotted out of it are those who have ignored and rejected the true God.

A similar scene to that of Revelation 20 is found in the book of Daniel. "As I looked, thrones were set in place, and the Ancient of Days took his seat. His clothing was white as snow; the hair of his head was white like wool. His throne was flaming with fire, and its wheels were all ablaze. A river of fire was flowing, coming out from before him. Thousands upon thousands attended him; ten thousand times ten thousand stood before him. The court was seated, and the books were opened." (Daniel 7:9-10)

The great and small

The reference to "the dead, great and small" in Revelation 20:12 teaches us that all humanity who had died, both the famous and the unknown, the rich and poor, the powerful and the insignificant, will be summoned to the final judgment. The worst outcome at this event would be to hear the declaration of condemnation by God, "I never knew you. Away from me, you evildoers!" (Matthew 7:23) The greatest outcome would be to hear God's words, "Well done, good and faithful servant ... Come and share your master's happiness!" (Matthew 25:21) There will be no greater joy than to know that we have pleased God in our service to him.

Dr. Henry Schaefer earned a doctorate in chemical physics from Stanford University and for 18 years served as professor of chemistry at the University of California. He eventually became director for the Center for Computational Quantum Chemistry at the University of Georgia. He authored more than 800 scientific publications and lectured at over 135 national and international scientific conferences. At one point, he was the sixth-most cited chemist out of some 628,000 chemists whose research was cited.

Yet Dr. Schaefer later said, "The most important discovery of my life was my discovery of Jesus Christ. I discovered the Jesus of history, the Jesus whose life is described on the pages of the New Testament."

This learned man, at one point virtually unequaled in his field of scientific expertise, found out that there was "no other" God than the One he met in Jesus. He will be among "the righteous," who will be affirmed and rewarded for their service to God at the final judgment.

Consider, too, the significance of that great Day in light of the story of Rogelio Leon. He was a soft-spoken young indigenous man who lived in an impoverished remote mountain town in Mexico where our family ministered for several years. He had become a believer in Christ through the witness of his godly mother and the preaching of several indigenous pastors. I had the privilege of helping to baptize him and others in a small pool along a mountain stream that ran through the valley. Rogelio grew in his faith and understanding of the Lord as he attended Bible studies we held for his family inside their simple log home.

However, he had one major problem; Rogelio was severely epileptic. His condition kept him from maturing normally, in that his speech was severely impeded, he had limited control of the movement of his body, and his personal hygiene was minimal. He never advanced beyond the level of a 10-year-old child, yet his parents lovingly cared for him. Rogelio also demonstrated a simple faith and had a joy of the Lord exceeding that of most others in the local evangelical church that his family attended.

A few years after we ended our work there, Rogelio was bathing in the stream one day, had a seizure, fell face down into the water, and drowned to death. It seemed to the believers in the area that God wanted to take him home. This man, virtually unknown to the outside world and unimpressive by any human standard, discovered the God of creation through faith in Christ—and he will join Dr. Schaefer on the Day of Judgment when believers of both the "great and small" will receive a warm welcome from their Lord and Savior.

Chapter 11

Immortality Revisited

Immortality is something that humans have sought for millennia, and the certainty of death has caused individuals, peoples, and whole cultures to look for a means of finding it. Many beliefs and practices have been developed throughout human history with the goal of attaining it—some simple and others quite elaborate. Even today people will use extreme methods such as cryogenics in their quest for it.

The ancient Egyptians, believed in immortality, but theirs was a system in which both the soul and body of kings and commoners alike could live forever as a result of following a complex series of ceremonies, preparations, and procedures. Because of their power and wealth, the pharaohs were able to ensure their own immortality by conscripting their subjects to perform the necessary rites and build the required dwellings to prepare them for the afterlife. The pyramids, and the tombs housed in them, are some of the greatest human-made monuments on Earth, demonstrating the lengths people will go to acquire immortality.

Tutankhamun, or King Tut, briefly reigned in Egypt around 1320 B.C. and was the most well-known pharaoh, in part because of the well-preserved objects and remains found centuries later inside his tomb. King Tut, who married his half-sister but could not by her produce an heir to succeed him as king, made the most ostentatious preparations for his death. Tut's embalmed body was covered with jewels, and a gold death mask weighing 23 pounds covered his face. A portion of the Egyptian Book of the Dead was inscribed on the back of the mask so that after death Tut could read the book's roadmap for the afterlife. The body lay inside three coffins, the first of pure gold and the others gilded, all of which were encased inside a larger stone sarcophagus surrounded by four gold-covered shrines. His monuments also included the tombs of other family members and the remains of their two unborn children. He must've thought if these couldn't usher him into the afterlife, nothing would!

To the Greek philosophers, however, the Egyptian system was totally unsatisfactory. Plato (428 B.C.) was the first major philosopher to develop the simple and more straightforward belief that the human *soul* was immortal. This meant that all humans, regardless of their status or adherence to any ritual or rite, were born immortal—so death was simply the release of the soul from the prison of the body. For him, the soul consisted of three parts: reason, spirit, and appetite. The soul was identified with the person and was not an impersonal collective consciousness (later, Neoplatonism taught that all souls eventually return to the "One" or the "Good" from which they emanated and from which all things originate). Many interpretations of Platonism pose not only an eternal soul but an everlasting universe, as opposed to it being created at a specific point in time.

Although the body could be destroyed, the ancient Greeks maintained that the soul of every person lived on forever after death. The Greek beliefs regarding judgment of the dead and the punishment of the wicked were extremely complex. Plato himself believed that the ultimate destination for the souls of virtuous people and heroes was a blessed paradise called Elysium, while the place of punishment of the souls of evil people was Tartarus. Souls who refused to enter Hades to be judged were thought to become ghosts, while those who did not receive a proper burial were believed to be covertly escorted into Hades in the dark of night. Souls of the wicked who were judged to be redeemable entered a sort of purgatory state after their first year of punishment. Some of these remnants of Greek mythology are still seen today in the doctrines of several Christian churches.

Because the human soul cannot be seen and is an abstract concept to many, it can be a difficult topic to discuss. Some people even deny that it exists. However, Jesus himself affirmed that the human soul does indeed exist and is separate from the body (Matthew 10:28, 16:26, and 22:37). Some Bible teachers divide the human into more than just body and soul. The command to love God with all our heart, soul, mind, and strength (Deuteronomy 6:5 and Matthew 22:37), and Paul's prayer for our "spirit, soul, and body" to be kept blameless (1 Thessalonians 5:23) suggest that what constitutes a human being can be divided into even more components. For the purpose of *Final Judgment & the Goodness of God,* it is sufficient to say that the soul is that component of ourselves that is not physical and that which makes each of us a unique person (similar to Plato's view only in this respect). Along with the body, the soul is what makes us who we are and distinguishes us from one another. Plus, to clarify, the spirit of a person is to be defined here as the breath of life which gives life to the body, breathed into each of us by the very breath of God.

The Platonic and Neoplatonic views of the human soul became engrained into Greek thought and much of ancient culture. Many of the Christian and even Muslim theologies developed over the ages have assumed and accommodated the view that the human soul is immortal and therefore indestructible. This belief affected many Christian theologies of hell so that the presupposition was that those who believe the gospel will spend eternity with God in heaven, while those that don't will spend eternity in hell.

In keeping with his adherence to Greek philosophy, Augustine forcefully maintained that the human soul cannot be destroyed; therefore, those that go to hell must survive there forever in some form. His descriptions of humans "living" in hell are bizarre and certainly may have terrified those living in the Middle Ages. The Roman Catholic Church later adopted Augustine's beliefs about the soul and hell, with Catholic theologians and philosophers incorporating these Greek philosophies into their teachings and elaborating on them. Thomas Aquinas, the influential Catholic priest and theologian of the 1200s, stated in his *Summa Theologica* that "eternity is the full, perfect and simultaneous possession of unending life."

Dante's *Inferno*[1] poetically described hell as a complex labyrinth of punishments for different kinds of sins, all of which go on forever. Nine circles of hell were reserved for those who committed different types of sins. The first circle was for non-Christians and pagans not evil enough to enter the lower circles, but who suffered in a temporary state in an inferior form of heaven called Limbo. The second circle was for those who were overcome by lust and therefore punished forever by strong violent winds, while the third was for gluttons who were forced to lie in a vile slush of icy rain. The fourth circle was for the greedy who were punished by having to use large weights to push against other greedy souls, while the fifth

---

1   Dante Alighieri, *Dante's Inferno*, The Divine Comedy (Book 1), Digireads.com, 2005.

circle was for those overcome by anger who were forced to forever fight against each other.

The sixth circle was for heretics (those who chose their own beliefs over those of the Pope and the Church), who were imprisoned in flaming tombs until judgment day when the tombs were then closed up and their souls and bodies sealed eternally in their flaming abode. The seventh circle was for the violent and those who committed suicide, blasphemy, and sodomy, while the eighth was for the fraudulent: seducers, sorcerers, false prophets, corrupt politicians, perjurers, hypocrites, and thieves. The final circle was set aside for those guilty of treachery. They were to be frozen in a lake of ice, with lower levels of the lake reserved for those who committed greater sins. Judas Iscariot was said to be confined at the lowest level.

Although *Inferno* was not thought of strictly as doctrine, it reflected the thinking of the people and the teaching of the Catholic Church at that time. Islam also adopted a form of the Augustinian view of hell, and put its own twist on how the wicked will suffer for countless ages in hell, but in different levels depending on the severity of the sins committed while on Earth. Some Islamic scholar's descriptions of hell are every bit as severe as those of Augustine, though some believe that the wicked will be released from hell after they have spent a specified time in suffering.

Protestant adaptions

The immortality of the soul and the unending conscious torment of the wicked in hell are doctrines that Martin Luther and other Protestant reformers did not touch since they had been engrained into the theology, culture, and languages of the Middle Ages. Protestant churches, therefore, adopted these beliefs and most Protestant denominations followed suit. Later creeds and theological statements such as the Westminster

Confession also incorporated eternal torment, though many Protestant theologies evolved that tried to soften the extent of suffering by using a more allegorical interpretation of hell.

The belief that humans are immortal is very alive in Christian churches today. It is very common to hear the statements, "We will all live forever, either in heaven or in hell," or "There are only two things on earth that are eternal: the Word of God and humans." Neither are not found in Scripture—yet they have been, and continue to be, proclaimed from the pulpit and in many popular books by Christian Bible teachers. One point of logic that should make anyone think twice before accepting this belief is that if the soul is really indestructible, then God cannot be fully sovereign, in that he would be prevented by some higher law from destroying something that he created. But since God *is* fully sovereign, then he can destroy anything that he has made since he is the One who assigns value and purpose to all that he creates. And, if it is true that the wicked will "live forever in hell," then they also have eternal life and cannot be really dead. A common explanation for this contradiction is that both the body and soul of the wicked will be resurrected for the final judgment, after which their body will be destroyed while their soul and spirit continue to live. But logically, the punishment must either be life with continual pain, or death, but not both.

The true biblical position of immortality is in total opposition to the Greek view. A quick study of the subject in Scripture yields far different conclusions. In fact, the few verses that specifically mention immortality don't even suggest that human souls are immortal from birth: "When the perishable has been clothed with the imperishable, and the mortal with immortality, then the saying that is written will come true: 'Death has been swallowed up in victory.'" (1 Corinthians 15:54) In this passage, immortality is associated with the resurrection of the dead. Death will be defeated at the resurrection, and the bodies of those who are resurrected as believers become immortal. The Apostle Paul also wrote of God's transcendent attributes in 1 Timothy 1:17, "Now to the King eternal, immortal, invisible, the only God, be honor and glory for ever and ever. Amen," while in 1 Timothy 6:15-16, he stated, "God, the blessed and only Ruler, the King of kings and Lord of lords, who alone is immortal, and who lives in unapproachable light, whom no one has seen or can see." This passage declares that *only* God is immortal, which by reason implies that human beings are not immortal, but mortal at birth.

That we are mortal is supported by how death came to the human race as recorded in Genesis. Adam and Eve were originally immortal, but after Adam had taken the forbidden fruit, God said, "The man has now become like one of us, knowing good and evil. He must not be allowed to reach out his hand and take also from the tree of life and eat, and live forever." (Genesis 3:22) God was not inclined to let evil and rebellious people live forever, so Adam and his wife were banished from the garden and prevented from eating of the tree of life which had previously made them immortal.

In Romans 2:7, the Apostle Paul states that those who receive eternal life are those who "seek glory, honor and immortality." If humans possessed immortality by birth, we would not need to seek it. Finally, Paul equated the promise of eternal life with immortality in 2 Timothy 1:9-10. He wrote, "This grace was given us in Christ Jesus before the beginning of time, but it has now been revealed through the appearing of our Savior, Christ Jesus, who has destroyed death and has brought life and immortality to light through the gospel." The apostle states that God's grace and true eternal life came to the human race through the gospel. The biblical view is that immortality is a gift from God, an expression of God's grace to those he saves from death. Immortality is not an automatic right, or the innate nature of all humans as Plato taught.

The position that humans become immortal only through the grace of God has more commonly been named "conditional immortality" by those that adhere to it, and is persuasively presented by John Stott in "Evangelical Essentials – A Liberal Evangelical Dialogue" and defended by John Wenham in his presentation, "Universalism and the Doctrine of Hell."

One objection raised against conditional immortality is Luke 20:34-36, where Jesus states that those who will experience the resurrection will not marry and do not die. But a deeper look at this passage reveals that Jesus is referring to "those who are considered worthy of taking part in that age and in the resurrection from the dead," "God's children," and "children of the resurrection," in other words, the redeemed. Since the wicked are not mentioned, this passage actually supports conditional immortality. If Jesus is saying that believers will be given immortality, then the converse, that the wicked will not, can safely be assumed. This is undeniably affirmed by Christ's declaration in Matthew 10:28: "Do not be afraid of those that kill the body but cannot kill the soul. Rather, be afraid of the One who can destroy both soul and body in hell."

Many believe today that those made in God's image are immortal as God is immortal, and God would never destroy someone that bears his image. Along with that, some use the term "infinite value of human life" with the reasoning that, since humans are immortal, made in God's image, and the pinnacle of God's creation, they are infinitely valuable. It cannot be denied that all human life starting from conception is valuable to God and given a high place in his universe, far exceeding that of animals. The sacrifice of his Son Jesus demonstrates how much God loves us and values us as humans. However, the idea that being made in God's image is connected to the immortality of the soul is not found anywhere in the Bible. Similarly, Scripture does not explicitly say that all humans are "infinitely" valuable. If this were literally true, then God's hands would be tied; he could never act in any way that violates our infinite worth, and therefore could never be fully sovereign.

In the end, it is more accurate to say that humans are *intrinsically* valuable, not infinitely so. Only one human, Jesus Christ who was both God and man, can be said to be "infinitely valuable," and through him we become God's dearly beloved. Next, we will explore in more depth the meaning of being made in God's image, and its implications for human existence.

Chapter 12

Made in the Image of God

As an unbeliever in the 1970s, I took several different roads to try to find God. Eastern religious thought and meditation was one road, which taught that I could achieve a state of inner peace and oneness with God by assuming a relaxed position and chanting my mantra, a procedure of repeating a word over and over again to produce the desired result.

But before long, I realized that this was like treating God as an impersonal force with no intelligence, emotion, or beauty. After a year of practicing this unfulfilling spiritual pursuit, I did not experience peace or oneness, and my chants and meditations started becoming more like prayers. Something inside me yearned for a relationship, not a procedure. At one point I pled, "God, please reveal yourself to me." That became the prayer I made to God almost every day.

A little time later, I was invited to a Christian fellowship on the University of Arizona campus where I was a student and began studying the Bible with several young Christian men. After being introduced to the claims of Jesus, I embraced the gospel—and a relationship with the living God through Christ was born. Instead of a procedure, prayer suddenly became conversation with a personal God, worship became passionate, and the study of God's Word came alive. Philosophical discussions became invigorating, interesting, and challenging, and science became awe-inspiring. As confirmation that I had found the truth, there were times I strongly sensed the presence of God, not just somewhere "out there," but in my life and indwelling my physical body. I felt an indescribable joy and peace from God's Spirit, and I knew that for the first time in my life I had come to experience the reason for which I was created: communion with the Creator.

This could only be possible because I was made in God's image (Genesis 1:27), like him so that I could relate to him personally. Because humans are like him, to some degree the very attributes of God can be seen in us. Although we worship God for his eternal characteristics, we can still marvel at the attributes that we share in common with God: personhood, reason and intelligence, love, understanding of a moral law, emotion, creativity, and appreciation of beauty. The human spirit in particular was created similar to that of God's Spirit, so that there could be communion between the two. God's desire is that we would know him and walk with him, and he created our spirit like his to allow this to happen. None of the other earthly creatures created by God have this privilege. When God's Spirit indwells and fills a person, there is intimate communication and connection between God and that person.

A.W. Tozer[1] understood this well, saying, "God formed us for His pleasure, and so formed us that we as well as He can in divine communion enjoy the sweet and mysterious mingling of kindred personalities. He meant us to see him and live with Him and draw our life from His smile."

Some have maintained that since animals also possess intelligence and emotion, those characteristics cannot be

---

1   A.W. Tozer, *The Pursuit of God*, CreateSpace Independent Publishing Platform, 2018.

attributed exclusively to the term "made in God's image." Others maintain that this term applies only to attributes such as holiness that were lost when Adam and Eve sinned. James 3:9-10 counters these views stating: "With the tongue we praise our Lord and Father, and with it we curse men, who have been made in God's likeness. Out of the same mouth come blessing and cursing. My brothers, this should not be." James's term, "God's likeness," is clearly interchangeable with "God's image", and "men" refers to all humans, not just believers in God. Therefore, people who curse those made in God's image are, by logic, degrading God himself. Furthermore, it makes sense that if Christ commands us to love God above all else, then we should also love those that were made like God; in fact, these are the two greatest commandments (Matthew 22:38-40). It is obvious that Christ was telling us to love not just those who are good and godly, but all who are made in God's image, in other words, all humans.

Those who seek God and submit to his will (the godly) reflect his image more fully, but all humans have retained God's image to some degree, even those who frequently don't demonstrate the character of God. As a result of sin, the attribute of moral knowledge was corrupted, but humans still retain a degree of awareness of right and wrong through their conscience. In fact, all of the attributes that we share with God were corrupted or degraded at the fall, but these characteristics still remain in all of us, not just those who are godly.

Just as James taught that we are not to use our spoken words to degrade those who are made in God's likeness, it is inconceivable that God would use his infinite powers to impose eternal and unending suffering on those he *made* in his own likeness. That would be the ultimate degradation. Christians generally affirm the sacredness of human life and the human soul, but prolonging God's punishment of the wicked into eternity does not affirm these values, but is an affront to them. It stands to reason, then, that completely ending the life of the wicked as portrayed in Matthew 10:28 is a compassionate judgment by God that affirms both his justice and the value of those he made in his image.

God's personal attributes

God did not make us in his image to somehow elevate us to his level, or suggest that we assumed his eternal nature from birth. He is the infinite God, and we are the finite creatures. Rather, God made us in his image so that we could have a person-to-person relationship with him. The attributes he possesses and created within us we possess finitely but he possesses infinitely, including reason, intelligence, a sense of justice, creativity, moral obligation, emotion, passion, and an appreciation of beauty. These attributes were designed to deepen, enhance, and solidify our relationship with God, and combined with a desire to know God, will move us toward him.

If we have reason and wisdom, then we also know that God is infinitely wise, so we can rely on him to lead us into greater wisdom and understanding than we could ever have on our own. If we are creative, then we know for certain that God is infinitely creative, and can trust him to inspire us to create even greater works for his glory. If we have emotion and passion, then we know that God is infinitely passionate, and we can depend on him to guide our emotions and to fill us with his passion by his indwelling Spirit to express our love for him and for others.

God is also exceedingly beautiful—and his beauty is one of the attributes that compels us to worship him (Psalm 27:4). Although no one has ever beheld the full beauty of the Lord, God has expressed a likeness of his beauty in the universe and nature, and has given us the capacity to acknowledge and appreciate it. When we do so and attribute it to the Creator, we express a most basic form of worship that gives us a point of contact with God that, to our knowledge, has not been given to the animals he made. Of course, when we create beauty in art or music, it is a dim but definite reflection of the infinite beauty of God.

If we have a sense of justice, then we know that God is infinitely just, so we can rely on him to show us where our judgments are lacking. If we have a sense of moral obligation, discerning right and wrong, then we know that God is infinitely righteous, and we can trust him to lead us down the correct path and keep us from sin. Our ability to know right from wrong is one of the main reasons why God can judge and punish us, as opposed to the animals who live and respond to their surroundings using their instincts.

Because we were created to have a personal relationship with God, he placed these personal attributes within us. But a relationship, by definition, must be mutual. Either individual can accept or reject the other. Since God has always maintained a position of welcome acceptance to all who come to him, if there is rejection, it is only on the part of the human, not God. One of the main questions that will be asked of each person at the final judgment will be, "Did you seek, accept, and embrace the Creator, or did you ignore, reject, or scorn him?" Or, put differently, did we use the attributes we share with God to move toward or away from him?

God's eternal attributes

The Greek view of the immortality of the human soul came in part because Greek philosophers did not see the greatness of the true Creator, or understand how wide the gap that exists between him and the human race. Not understanding the infinite attributes of the true God, Greek gods were more like people than the Creator. Therefore, they attributed human characteristics to their gods and godlike characteristics to humans.

God's eternal attributes of transcendence, sovereignty, immortality, omnipresence, omniscience, and omnipotence are reserved only for him. These attributes are the very reason that we worship God since they belong only to God and no one else. Before God created us and gave us life, we didn't exist, so we were never immortal from the beginning. We came into existence by his sovereign will—and we are totally dependent on him for life, since he alone sustains us and gives us the right of our existence.

Although only God possesses immortality, he gives immortality to us as he pleases as a gift, as the previously quoted 2 Timothy 1:9-10 declares, God "has saved us and called us to a holy life—not because of anything we have done but because of his own purpose and grace. This grace was given us in Christ Jesus before the beginning of time, but it has now been revealed through the appearing of our Savior, Christ Jesus, who has destroyed death and has brought life and immortality to light through the gospel." Because he created us for the purpose of an eternal relationship with him, God allows us to enter his realm of eternity through grace. This magnificent truth is one of the core messages of the gospel.

Near the close of the Gospel that bears his name, the Apostle John said it was written "that you may believe that Jesus is the Christ, the Son of God, and that by believing you may have life in his name." (John 20:31) The Greek word used here for "life" is *zoe*, which in this passage refers to *God's* life, the eternal, unchanging life of God himself. It is this life that is given us through his Spirit, the same Spirit that comes to dwell in those who come to faith in Christ. It is through the presence of this *zoe* life that we are made immortal and fit to live with God forever after the final judgment. As Ephesians 1:13-14 affirms, "Having believed, you were marked in him with a seal, the promised Holy Spirit, who is a deposit guaranteeing our inheritance until the redemption of those who are God's possession—to the praise of his glory."

It's a glorious reality! Because we are made in God's image, his personal and eternal attributes combine to give us our substance, draw us to him, and enable us to have the opportunity to dwell with him forever, even as he dwells in us through his Spirit. It's what I discovered and experienced as a young man in college, and it remains what I proclaim today.

Chapter 13

The Justice of God

As a young Christian, I attended a number of evangelical churches of various denominations and was exposed to different theologies of the end times, the final judgment and punishment, and God's justice. Over time, I noticed that churches, Bible teachers, and Christian subcultures had divergent views on these issues, many of which we've explored previously. Although none overtly rejected any specific scripture related to the final judgment, most had preferred verses to support their opinions and also seemed to ignore some Bible passages while emphasizing others. Because there was no obvious consensus, I did not develop a strong commitment to any position back then—and like most of my Christian friends, did not feel a need to do so.

I have since realized that these topics are vital not just because we need to have correct theology, but because God's reputation is at stake. A distorted picture of the one who made us in his image gives the unbelieving world reason to reject the gospel and malign Christ's followers as well as God himself. Most believers assume the final punishment will more resemble that described by Augustine, and I've found it negatively affects their view of God.

The Lord is a loving God, but a faulty view of justice impedes that understanding. It is evident that human concepts of love and justice are frequently in conflict with each other, but the truth is that God's love and justice are in complete harmony with one another, and it's through a fuller understanding of the final judgment that we can come to understand that relationship.

In general, humans do not know the meaning of justice. Usually, we'll wish severe punishment on our enemies but a light punishment for ourselves. Some of us have completely lost our sense of justice and view any punishment as unjust. But the Lord is just because he is fair and punishes sin equitably, so the severity of God's punishment will always match the severity of the sin. I'd never want another human to determine my eternal punishment or reward; rather, I'll take God's judgment since it's fairer than any human's ruling. The Lord is infinitely just, but is unwilling to punish, for he doesn't want "anyone to perish, but everyone to come to repentance." (2 Peter 3:9)

One of the justifications for Augustine's unending conscious torment of the wicked in hell cited by some preachers today is that God is a just God. To them, God's justice means that he is somehow obligated to be severe. In this view, justice trumps the character of God so that his punishment inevitably involves being unbearably harsh with sinners at the expense of his love. This is rationalized, they say, since after the final judgment God is kind and loving to the believers. This dichotomy of God's love on one side and the exceedingly severe justice on the other is difficult for many to embrace, even Christians. But as we've already learned, it is not necessary to embrace it.

The Augustinian teachings on judgment went unquestioned in the Middle Ages largely because the medieval mind was inclined to envision a much more harsh and vindictive God than was presented in Scripture. Roman Catholic Church leaders effectively used these teachings to frighten people into accepting the Church's authority so that they could avoid hell. Many who advocated the eternal conscious torment of the wicked then assumed that God must punish sin at least as severely as *they* could envision, and probably much more.

Proponents of the unending conscious torment view today reply that sin is much more serious and horrible to God than to us, and so such torment demonstrates God's hatred for sin. They also claim that this proclaims God's glory and proves his sovereignty and power. Yet how long should it take for God to prove that he hates sin? Certainly not an eternity. God does not have to repeat a punishment over and over to prove any point he wants to make. Plus, why does God necessarily need to prove anything to anyone? His will is supreme. He answers to no one. "He does whatever pleases him." (Psalm 115:3) It is universally accepted that God is all powerful and there is none who can claim to be his equal. Why would God ever want to "prove" his power by tormenting the poor and weak earthly creatures that he himself created? This portrays God as vain and pathetic.

Another objection to this logic is that an eternity of suffering is not a just punishment for a limited amount of sin committed during a person's lifetime. Nowhere in Scripture does God require more for our sin than is reasonable and just. Throughout the Old Testament, the idea is presented that the punishment should match the crime, whether individual offenses or crimes committed by the nation of Israel as a whole. Punishment by an eternity of suffering and excruciating pain is not a just punishment for a few decades of rebellion on Earth. That punishment does not match the crime. What system of justice punishes someone who has committed a specific crime of limited duration with an eternity of retribution? Even our society's life sentences cannot come close to that level of retribution. By any measure, this is intrinsically *unjust*. This even suggests that God hates sin so much that he actually loses control when punishing sinners and in a fit of anger inflicts the greatest amount of damage possible. That is utterly inconsistent with God's character as revealed in Scripture. Christopher Marshall[1] presents strong arguments against retribution as God's means for balancing the scales of justice and the injustice of an eternity of conscious torment as God's final punishment for the wicked.

A lifetime of opportunity

The degree of severity of God's punishment on the wicked is not based on God's power, greatness, or importance, but on the fact that the wicked have been given a lifetime of opportunity to seek God and his love, yet have not responded. Therefore, at the end of their lives they have no further purpose or role in God's plan. The Lord does not need to prove anything in punishing the wicked and finds no joy in it. Still, there are some who say, "God's ways are higher than our ways, so we can't understand them but just have to accept them by faith." This reasoning, however, ignores the fact that their understanding of God's "ways" in Scripture could be wrong, that God has gone to great lengths in the Bible to show that he is kind and compassionate, and that he doesn't like it when humans go the wrong way, but delights when we seek him and find the right path. He rewards obedience and discourages disobedience whenever possible. As

---

1   Christopher Marshall, *Beyond Retribution*, Eerdmans, 2001.

Christopher Marshall[2] aptly stated, God's ways are higher than our ways, not lower.

Sadly, the phrase "God's ways are not our ways" has been used by some preachers to advocate spurious ideas not found in the Bible and to teach doctrines that are illogical and contradictory. The context of the actual passage is one where the thoughts and ways of the wicked are contrasted with those of God. "Seek the Lord while he may be found; call on him while he is near. Let the wicked forsake his way and the evil man his thoughts. Let him turn to the Lord, and he will have mercy on him, and to our God, for he will freely pardon. 'For my thoughts are not your thoughts, neither are your ways my ways,' declares the Lord. As the heavens are higher than the earth, so are my ways higher than your ways and my thoughts than your thoughts." (Isaiah 55:6-9) The thoughts of God concern the condition of those entrapped and condemned by their own sin, and the ways of God are mercy, forgiveness, and restoration because of his love for the sinner. Conversely, the thoughts and ways of the wicked do not look out for the good of others but delight in seeing the downfall and punishment of people, especially their enemies. The fact that every human has behaved in this way at one time or another shows that God's ways are *indeed* higher than ours—so we are commanded to seek God and his forgiveness so that we can escape our wicked ways and be delivered from our evil thoughts.

Justice is not well understood by most people, either secular or religious. Those from modern secular cultures in Europe and the U.S. have an aversion to even the concepts of punishment and retribution. This is why many Christians today are reluctant to discuss the final judgment with non-believers. In addition, they simply cannot defend such an illogical proposition as the eternal conscious torment of the wicked,

---

2   Ibid.

and are embarrassed to try. Certain fearless open-air preachers who forcefully threaten people from street corners or college squares with eternal hellfire and damnation are the few brave (and foolish) enough to boldly preach this doctrine. But if the Augustinian view of hell was really true, then everyone should be warning people about it since an eternity of excruciating pain and continual suffering is something anyone would avoid, no matter what the price.

The Bible asserts in many passages that because God is the only true judge of humanity, we are commanded not to judge others. "There is only one Lawgiver and Judge, the one who is able to save and destroy. But you—who are you to judge your neighbor?" (James 4:12). By passing judgment on others, we insert ourselves into the place and authority of God himself, a ludicrous position for anyone to take. But even in religious societies, God's justice is also frequently misrepresented or twisted, and prejudging the innocent can be common. It has been said that Satan's crowning achievement is the use of religion and religious people to promote his agenda of evil, injustice, and hatred.

Asia Bibi, a woman from rural Pakistan, was working in the berry fields when she went to get a drink of water from the community well. Her co-workers, because they were Islamic and she was Christian, accused her of defiling the water with her cup. Her reply was, "I don't believe that Mohammed would share the same view as you." According to one account, Asia was accused of blasphemy for her statement, and then tried and condemned. Under Pakistan's new blasphemy law, the crime of insulting Mohammed is punishable by death, so in 2010 she was sentenced to death by hanging. During her imprisonment, the Pakistani minister of minorities and a Pakistani governor who defended her were assassinated by enraged Muslim extremists. After the Pakistani Supreme

Court acquitted her in 2018, her persecutors still demanded her death, protesting in the streets and enflaming much of their nation, effectively keeping her from being able to leave the country. But in claiming to represent God's justice, they have put themselves in great peril. "For in the same way you judge others, you will be judged, and with the measure you use, it will be measured to you." (Matthew 7:2) On the day of God's justice, the wicked who judged others will be judged by their own standards, and those that unjustly condemned others will themselves be irreversibly condemned.

Predestination of the wicked

The word "predestination" is a distinctly biblical word. To most Christians, the term refers to the belief that God pre-ordained believers to be formed into the image of Christ, taken from Romans 8:29: "For those God foreknew he also predestined to be conformed to the likeness of his Son, that he might be the firstborn among many brothers." Some also take Ephesians 1:11 to apply to God's sovereign choice in choosing those that are to be saved. Speaking of Jesus, it says, "In him we were also chosen, having been predestined according to the plan of him who works out everything in conformity with the purpose of his will." Although all Christians accept the concept of God's sovereignty, there is some disagreement as to how far God allows us to exercise our free will and how that affects our eternal destiny.

One particularly harmful theology is the teaching of pre-destination coupled with the unending conscious torment of the wicked in hell. Combined, it states that God not only chooses those who will be saved, but also those who will suffer in hell. This view was held by some in the Middle Ages and developed more fully during the Reformation, and is held today by those adhering to an extreme form of Calvinism.

Their chain link theology progresses to say that, since hell is real and people who don't have salvation go there, and since people who are not Christians don't have salvation, then non-Christians are predestined to burn in hell forever. This includes, they claim, children of non-believers not old enough to understand the gospel.

According to this twisted logic, God, in his sovereignty, created most of humanity for the ultimate purpose of tormenting them in hell forever. This somehow demonstrates God's glory by displaying man's wickedness in contrast to God's righteousness. Those whom God has saved will observe God's justice through his punishment of the condemned into eternity. This also divides humanity into two unalterable groups, as assigned by God at birth: the saved and the damned.

There are many weak links within this theological chain, and each one makes the formula increasingly toxic. First, the term "predestined" is used four times in the New Testament and only for those who are believers in Christ, and not for the wicked. Second, a loving God would not throw people into hell to be tortured forever who had not had a chance to respond to his offer of salvation. That sounds more like something that the devil would do, and it was likely the devil himself that inspired these teachings to slander the name and character of God so that people do not love him or trust him, but run from him in fear and loathing. Third, there are countless passages in the Bible where God exhorts the wicked to seek him and repent so that they can find salvation. Ezekiel 33:11 proclaims, "As surely as I live, declares the Lord, I take no pleasure in the death of the wicked, but rather that they turn from their ways and live. Turn! Turn from your evil ways!" But if this extreme view of predestination is true, then all offers of forgiveness and salvation by God to the wicked are insincere and even unnecessary since he has already predetermined at birth who will be saved and who will be damned.

If there was ever a doctrine designed to lead people away from God's love, it is this one. This drives unbelievers away from the gospel, not to it; they look at this belief as crazy and held by narrow, hateful, and self-righteous people. They reason that if this doctrine is a reflection of the nature of the Christian God and of those who follow him, then this is a God they would never believe in. For many, it even provides a reason to not believe in the existence of God at all.

The Lord wants all people to understand him and know him (1 Timothy 2:3-4) so that we can draw near to him and worship him as the great and wonderful God he is, and not the distorted, slanderous image of him the devil has implanted in human minds. God is truly loving and kind, and when punishment of sin is inevitable, he punishes fairly and justly.

Eternal torture

Augustine, and preachers both throughout history and today, have taught that God tortures unbelievers forever. Many modern churches use the noun "torment" in their formal statements of faith when discussing the fate of the wicked, and while it has a milder connotation than torture, the basic meaning is the same. Although the vast majority of Christians will say they do not believe God would intentionally torment anyone for eternity, they also don't seem to understand that the Augustinian view of hell they may subscribe to demands such a conclusion.

One of the passages frequently used to support this view of God causing unending torture is the parable of the unmerciful servant in Matthew 18:23-35. In it, Jesus tells the story of a servant who was forgiven of a great debt by his master, but then goes out and throws someone in jail for not being able to pay him back for a much lesser debt. In verse 34, the master turned this servant "over to the jailers to be tortured" until he paid back everything that was originally owed.

Yet remember what we learned earlier about parables in the Bible: they have to be interpreted in context. J. Robertson McQuilken[3] provided a good treatment on how to properly interpret parables. Two of the most important rules he cited are that parables are meant to illustrate only one or two main spiritual principles, and not everything in a parable is theologically significant. The main thrust of the parable of the unmerciful servant is that God commands us to forgive one another just as he forgave us. The fact that the jailers in the story practiced torture does not mean Jesus was advocating torture or saying that God himself tortures people. The story does teach that God will punish those who are unforgiving, but the method of punishment is certainly not the focus, nor was it intended to be. Parables are full of metaphors, and the torture by the jailers in this parable is probably a metaphor for the anguish and suffering that unforgiving people experience, both now and possibly at the final judgment. If it does refer to the latter, it is clear that it is limited in duration, and certainly not eternal, since the punishment takes place until the servant paid back everything that was originally owed.

Revelation 20, a Bible chapter already cited often in this book, records the future punishment of the devil, the beast, and the false prophet (the three supernatural enemies of God) as being thrown into the lake of fire, saying "they will be tormented day and night forever and ever." (Revelation 20:10) Although some disagree, Satan himself might not be totally destroyed at the end of human history, but will be preserved to exist forever and be tormented because of the

---

3   J. Robertson McQuilken, *Understanding and Applying the Bible*, Moody Publishers, New edition, 2009.

great sin he committed against God. But the mention of "day and night" might also suggest that this torment will last only as long as day and night exist; in other words, not for eternity. This verse, though, has also been used to argue that humans will also be tormented in hell forever. The reasoning is that whatever Satan suffers will also be experienced by the wicked because the location, the lake of fire, is the same for both. Whatever the correct interpretation of this verse, it is clear that only the devil, the beast, and the false prophet are being tormented day and night forever, not people. In the account of the final punishment of those humans whose names were not found in the book of life (Revelation 20:15), the language used was simply "thrown into the lake of fire." Eternal torture is not mentioned.

It must be asked: "What purpose would possibly be served for God to continually torment someone forever?" While the benefits of torture as a means of gathering information from an enemy combatant during wartime can be debated, it has been rejected by most societies today. Some have even used torture as a deterrent, believing that when people know it will be the punishment, they will capitulate and choose freedom over pain and suffering. Such was the case for European leaders in the Middle Ages. They had no problem with torture, using it commonly to extract confessions, instill fear to try to keep others from committing crimes, or, in some cases, to inflict maximum pain during capital punishments. Torture was often used by the Inquisition on "heretics" who disagreed with teachings of the Catholic Church. It was sometimes used by civil authorities as a punishment for lesser crimes under the assumption it might cause criminals to repent and thus avoid the much greater punishment of being thrown into hell to be tormented by God forever.

Medieval methods of punishment were extremely cruel and sadistic, designed to inflict maximum pain or prolong suffering prior to death. Mutilation and burning were common. "Ordeal by fire" and "ordeal by water"—the burning of the flesh in fire or the scorching of the flesh by boiling water—were used as a method to determine guilt. If a person was innocent, it was believed God would intervene and begin healing the accused after three days. If the wounds did not show improvement, then the person was pronounced guilty. Burning at the stake was a common punishment used for those guilty of capital crimes such as murder, heresy, and sometimes theft. Stocks (where the feet were bound in a wooden frame) and pillory (where both hands and the head were similarly bound) were used to humiliate those charged with lesser crimes. However, these were sometimes combined with the burning of the hands and feet while the person was trapped and unable to move.

The use of torture reached its peak in the twelfth century but continued even into the eighteenth century, and different methods were developed. They included being heated alive inside a brass bull; being fastened to a rack which stretched the victim's body to where ligaments were torn and limbs came out of joint; and the iron maiden, a hinged coffin with internal spikes that pierced the body as it was closed. There was also the breaking wheel that was rolled over the victim, shattering their body before the person was left to die. In some cases, the body was stretched over the wheel itself and the bones were broken by clubs.

It is unimaginable that these methods of punishment were actually used. Yet knowledge of this unsavory history is necessary to understand the connection between the medieval view of justice and medieval theology of hell. To a large degree, medieval methods of torture reflected the people's beliefs on how God punishes the wicked in hell, as originally derived from the Greek view of Hades.

Today, torture as a means of punishment is universally considered vindictive, vengeful, sadistic, and inhumane. This type of torture does not serve any positive purpose and is not effective for teaching a lesson, or convincing anyone of anything. It is much more likely that the victim of torture will develop an intense hatred for the torturer and an even more fervent hatred for his enemies.

The concept of torture as a deterrent to keep people from hell is now practically non-existent. The vast majority of people who choose a destructive path in life don't necessarily believe that God will punish them at all, much less through an eternity of torture. That's because most people don't believe in hell, and for unbelievers in particular, the thought that God would torture someone as punishment is unthinkable. All Christians can agree that the sadistic, evil, and inhumane killings by ISIS in Iraq and Syria from 2014-2017 was from the devil, and not from God. But it is strange that Christians could also believe that God, because he is just, could inflict humans with a torture far more painful and which lasts for eternity.

God cannot act in a way that contradicts his own moral code, one that he has also imposed on humans. Therefore, believers should ask, "Why would God, who commands us to love our enemies, torture his own enemies without ceasing into eternity?" All believers throughout history have confessed that God is just, but God is also *good*, and his justice does not eclipse his goodness. He resolved this apparent conflict over justice and goodness through the death of Jesus. Christ's sacrifice brought the two together, with God's justice satisfied at Christ's expense; he took the punishment for us. And thus God remains both good and just.

The idea that God would torture humans in hell for eternity is not found in Scripture, is not worthy of God's name, and does not reflect God's character.

Chapter 14

Popular Views of the Final Punishment

Possibly the most popular belief today in our culture about the final punishment is that it is the eternal separation from God, but nothing more. This view seems to be supported by the biblical truth that sinners choose to live separately from God, and that this state continues after their deaths. However, when combined with the Greek view of the immortality of the human soul, it again takes the position that the final punishment continues forever.

Many who hold to this idea reason that separation from God is a much greater punishment than anything we can imagine, so Scripture uses fire as a metaphor to describe the unbearable pain of being isolated from God. This is nothing more, though, than another attempt to soften the idea of Augustine's eternal unending torture in hell—with the torture, in this case, not being caused by God, but by the fact that the person is now conscious of their separation from God and can do nothing to remedy it.

Separation only

The eternal separation only view is taken primarily from

the twice-before mentioned parable of the talents (Matthew 25:14-30) where Jesus described the fateful end of the one servant that did not invest the talent that was given him, saying in verse 30, "Throw that worthless servant outside, into the darkness, where there will be weeping and gnashing of teeth." But, knowing what we've already learned about the interpretation of parables, this story illustrates a spiritual lesson and is by definition filled with metaphors. In keeping with the story line, it was very natural in ancient times that upon returning home and discovering an unfaithful and irresponsible servant of a household, an owner would throw that servant out from the premises, even at nighttime if necessary. The "darkness" into which the irresponsible servant is thrown is a metaphor for the punishment that awaits the wicked, not a literal description of an everlasting place of isolation from God.

Also associated with this view is the passage from 2 Thessalonians 1:9 which states that unbelievers will be "punished with everlasting destruction and shut out from the presence of the Lord." The conclusion from the latter part of this verse that the final punishment is only eternal separation from God ignores the earlier context of the passage, which strongly suggests that the wicked will be separated from God as a result of the destruction; they do not exist in some dark state of the soul that continues forever.

A modern-day literary version of this belief is portrayed in C.S. Lewis's *The Great Divorce*,[1] written in part to rebut a famous poem by William Blake entitled "The Marriage of Heaven and Hell." Blake argued that while Christians claimed that hell was wicked and should be avoided at all costs, hell and even evil were necessary for there to be creativity, enlightenment, and happiness. Blake's poem claimed that the path to

---

1   C.S. Lewis, *The Great Divorce*, HarperOne; Revised edition, 2015.

human enlightenment was a marriage of heaven and hell in our lives—to be kind and lawful but also proud and devious.

To refute Blake's view, Lewis permanently "divorces" heaven and hell by poetically describing a bus trip of those who are dead from "grey town" (a picture of the dwelling place of the wicked) to heaven and then back again. Since everything is so real and beautiful in heaven, the travelers discover that they are not fit to live there, and instead out of fear return to "grey town," where they remain in their ghostlike state forever, mistrusting and hating everyone else and eternally drifting apart from each other and God. For them, the town was only a temporary place of transition (or purgatory). Although Lewis is widely read and greatly respected, *The Great Divorce* is fiction and its ideas and images are speculative and should be considered literary and poetic license, not doctrine.

Although *The Great Divorce* assumes the immortality of the human soul, Lewis expresses beliefs more sympathetic with the destruction view of the final punishment in his book *The Problem of Pain*.[2] "I notice that Our Lord, while stressing the terror of hell with unsparing severity, usually emphasises the idea, not of duration, but of finality. Consignment to the destroying fire is usually treated as the end of the story—not as the beginning of a new story. That the lost soul is eternally fixed in its diabolical attitude we cannot doubt. But whether this eternal fixity implies endless duration—or duration at all—we cannot say." When written in 1940, the fashion of the day was to adhere to the Augustinian view of hell, but Lewis nonetheless expressed his doubts about it openly and read Scripture as he saw it, not as others expected him to read it.

A commonly heard phrase spoken today when someone dies is that they "pass into eternity." For some, the term means that the deceased enter an eternal state that goes on forever.

---

2   C.S. Lewis, *The Problem of Pain*, HarperOne; Revised edition, 2015.

This is true for those of us who are Christians, and I believe the first thing we are aware of after we die is the start of our existence in everlasting fellowship with God. "For to me, to live is Christ and to die is gain ... I desire to depart and be with Christ, which is better by far." (Philippians 1:21, 23) However, those who are without faith in God upon death await judgment in some intermediate state (possibly Hades), but their final destiny is realized after the final judgment— and although the outcome of that judgment is eternal, their soul is not.

The final punishment of the wicked is separation from God forever by the ultimate destruction by him of their body and soul. Since they will remain in their spiritually dead state at the judgment, without love for God, it is doubtful that they will be in anguish over the fact that they are being separated from him. It is much more likely they will be in agony over the prospect of having to face God and then exist in a state of opposition to him forever, knowing they can never escape. Instead of desiring to be closer to God at the final judgment, they will probably recoil from his presence and want nothing to do with him. They'll likely wish they were completely dead; in other words, destroyed, and that's exactly what God, in his compassion, will do for them.

Do people send themselves to hell?

One day I turned on the radio in my car and listened to a program featuring a popular preacher. He was teaching about hell, and at one point he stated that hell was not made for humans but only for the devil and his angels. He went on to say that people were never supposed to have been there, but choose to go to hell. His teaching was based in part on the statement made by Jesus in Matthew 25:41, which says, "Then he will say to those on his left, 'Depart from me, you who are cursed, into the eternal fire prepared for the devil and his angels.'"

As I listened, I thought, *How do people end up in hell that are never supposed to be there? Does God know about this?* Then I mused, *If God does know about it, then perhaps he lost control of the process at some point.* As the teaching progressed, I got the impression that the preacher was not totally comfortable with what he was saying, but felt he had to teach it since he was convinced that it was in the Bible.

This view is popular in many Christian circles and amounts to a kind of apology for hell, which is especially necessary if one holds to the eternal conscious torment of the wicked. The statement that hell was prepared for the devil and his angels is a true statement and forms the first link in this theological chain. The second link is the claim that hell was not prepared for people, a suspicious assertion since Jesus did not say that. Then, as the argument goes, God never really intended for people to go to hell (the third and very weak link), but because those that reject the truth are *choosing* to go there, God has no choice but to allow them to do so. At this point, the argument becomes ridiculous.

The numerous warnings by Jesus throughout the Gospels about the imminent destruction of those that rebel against God, combined with the reality of God's overriding sovereignty in judgment, are more than enough to dispel this view. The belief that Gehenna was not prepared for wicked humanity misses the whole point of Christ's teaching, that the eternal fire is being prepared to completely burn up whatever is thrown into it. God's ultimate plan is to ultimately destroy evil and all evildoers. Isaiah 26:10-11 clearly refutes the notion that hell was not prepared for the wicked. It declares, "Though grace is shown to the wicked, they do not learn righteousness; even in a land of uprightness they go on doing evil and regard not the majesty of the Lord. O Lord, your hand is lifted high, but they do not see it. Let them see your zeal for your people and be put to shame; let the fire reserved for your enemies consume them."

Of course, there are those who believe a punishment is fair only if those being punished fully understand the nature of their punishment well in advance. There are also many Bible teachers that say God gives all people plenty of warning about hell, so if they end up there they have no one to blame but themselves—and, in a sense, are therefore choosing to go there. Yet this is true only for those who have heard accurate Bible teachings about hell, and we already know most people either have no belief in, or are totally ignorant of, God's future judgment. Most Christian church pastors don't preach about, much less discuss, God's final punishment, and much of what congregants hear is erroneous. But in spite of all this, God's hands are not tied. A complete and accurate description to the wicked about their final punishment is not necessary for him to execute justice. We can be assured that on judgment day he will punish the ungodly fairly and justly regardless of their beliefs about or knowledge of hell. And the idea that all those who end up in hell consciously choose to go there is false. The majority of those who are punished in Gehenna have been deceived into thinking that no such punishment exists, they are not deserving of it, or they simply don't care.

It is also doubtful that the fear of hell itself is of much value to a person unless it leads them to a love for God. Those who enter into eternal life are those who have sought and found God, who love God, and have been cleansed from sin so that they are fit to live with God. Those who only fear punishment but have no love for God are not fit to live with him because, as 1 John 4:18 tells us, "There is no fear in love. But perfect love drives out fear, because fear has to do with punishment. The one who fears is not made perfect in love."

People don't end up in hell by default. The scenes in Matthew 25 and Revelation 20 do not in any way portray a God who is placidly allowing people to go into Gehenna, but shows him presiding over the judgment. It is God who commands his angels to carry out the horrific sentence and punishment. Jesus's parables illustrate what will take place for the wicked immediately after the sentence of condemnation is pronounced: rejection, anger, disputing with God over his judgment and sentence, despair, temporary suffering, crying, resistance, and gnashing of teeth. The gnashing is not necessarily an expression of pain, but of rage against God and possibly a suggestion they will resist their punishment.

This scene, of course, has been repeated countless times in human history, where people have appeared before an earthly judge expecting to receive a favorable outcome, only to be told that they have no case or to find the judgment given in favor of their opponent. Anger, crying, and threats against the judge are all common responses. There are even a significant number of cases of physical violence breaking out in the courtroom. According to "Off the Record,"[3] during a custody hearing in Las Vegas, Nevada in December 2006, 36-year-old Geoffrey Wells was attending a hearing after his 12-year-old son had killed himself with one of Wells' unlocked and loaded guns. The judge held him responsible, and he was so outraged at the judge's decision that he began attacking the bailiffs in the courtroom. It took ten bailiffs to subdue him, four of which required medical attention. Wells was sentenced to six months in jail and was denied custody of his other children.

On judgment day, there will also be many who are totally surprised that God pronounces condemnation and judgment

---

3   Blog by Mark Harris posted at www.CRSchools.net.

on them, as they firmly believed they deserved to enter heaven because they were innocent of any grave sin, lived a good life, or had done great things in the name of God (Matthew 7:21-23). They will be enraged that God would unfairly pronounce such a judgment on them. But Jesus' final words to them will be "I never knew you."

Chapter 15

Death and Resurrection

It's been said that death is the great leveler. No one escapes its appointment; all must pass through its door. What lies beyond death is a subject of great concern to us all and has fascinated humans for eons; but there are as many explanations as there are philosophies and religions. Some come close to the truth, while others land far from it, but all cannot possibly be right. There are some who profess to have entered its realm, only to return. Although we cannot categorically disprove their claims, there is good reason to doubt some of them.

Yet Christians declare to have access to the greatest wisdom and knowledge available concerning death and the afterlife, as well as a personal and permanent relationship with the One who conquered death itself.

Death and spiritual legacy

King Solomon wrote some of the most profound statements about death. One in particular challenges us all to stop and ponder. "A good name is better than fine perfume, and the day of death better than the day of birth. It is better to go to a house of mourning than to go to a house of feasting, for death is the destiny of every man; the living should take this to heart." (Ecclesiastes 7:1-2) Death makes us think about what is really important in life—things greater than ourselves, and those that are eternal.

The death of someone forces those who knew them to consider the positive or negative impact they had on others. A "good name" results from a legacy that was positive. Out of respect, most memorial services emphasize the positive qualities of the deceased, though each person present will have an opinion of how they were affected by the person. If it was negative, they will likely keep it to themselves. Regardless, once a person dies, their name is established with the people who knew them. If the deceased has a checkered past or a questionable faith, even though kind words may be said about them, the negative memories remain.

Such was not the case for Carol Hungerford, my wife's mother. For most of her life, Carol was a committed Christian, a woman of grace and faith, and her life was filled with good deeds and her mouth with kind words toward others that reflected the thoughts of God. She served the Lord and spent much of her time helping others know God's love and his Word. The service memorializing her life was attended by many people, believers and non-believers alike, including some international students my wife and I befriended. I had the privilege of giving a eulogy at the gravesite. As I acknowledged Carol's life of faith and service, there was no awkwardness or hesitation, and no need for half-truths or exaggerations. Her good name was clearly established with those present, and there was no doubt in anyone's mind that the words I spoke about her were true. The well-known passages written by King Solomon in Ecclesiastes 7 about death were then read, but not to benefit Carol; she was with God. It was the living, those who could still choose to love and serve God and others as Carol did, to whom the verses were addressed.

Even more important than the heritage of our earthly name when we die is the fact that our name has also been established before God. It is our name, which represents the totality of our lives and record of our deeds, our "spiritual legacy," that will be reviewed at the final judgment. To those who trusted in God, Jesus promised, "I will never blot out his name from the book of life, but will acknowledge his name before my Father and his angels." (Revelation 3:5) The names of all who loved and served God will be recognized by the Lord on judgment day and will remain in God's book of life forever. Death can never touch them again! But all of the worthless and evil endeavors that were pursued on Earth by the wicked, as well as the unfruitful work of the righteous, will be seen for what they are and will all go up in smoke. For the unrighteous, the day will be a complete disappointment and a total loss, as they will have no legacy before God. As Psalm 112:6, 9-10 declares, "A righteous man will be remembered forever ... his righteousness endures forever; his horn will be lifted high in honor. The wicked will see and be vexed, he will gnash his teeth and will waste away."

Three deaths

In his letter to the Roman church, the Apostle Paul stated that "the wages of sin is death." (Romans 6:23) Death is described in Genesis when God warned Adam and Eve of the forbidden fruit, "When you eat of it you will surely die." (Genesis 2:17) Although the first couple did not die physically immediately after partaking of the fruit, God's presence—the *zoe* life of God—was taken from their bodies and they died spiritually that day. The fellowship they had with God and the life they continually received from him were severed. Physical death

149

came later. Since that event, every human has been born into spiritual and physical death.

There are three types of death referred to in the Bible: spiritual death, physical death, and final death. Commentators have noted that these specific terms are not found in Scripture, and the single word "death" is used for all three types. However, as you study the Bible more deeply, you become aware that the word death is used in many ways throughout Scripture with varying components emphasized in different passages. For example, spiritual death is clearly referenced in Ephesians 2:1, which says, "As for you, you were dead in your transgressions and sins," while the death mentioned in Revelation 20:6 refers to the final death: the destruction of both body and soul in Gehenna. As stated previously, the word "perish" is used in many cases to refer only to physical death, but in the Gospel of John it refers to the death of the whole person accomplished by destruction. (John 3:16) The conclusion of John's discussion on eternal life states, "Whoever believes in the Son has eternal life, but whoever rejects the Son will not see life." (John 3:36) In other words, those that reject God's provision of salvation through Christ will experience the total absence of life, which is death.

In keeping with the Greek and Augustinian view of the human soul, many Bible commentators and teachers define death only as "separation." Physical death then becomes defined as the separation of the soul from the body since the soul is assumed to live on forever (following Plato's view), while spiritual death is defined simply as the soul's separation from God. Both definitions are based on theological assumptions; however, the obvious and universally understood meaning of death is simply the end of life.

It is true that physical death involves the soul's separation from the body, but this separation is the *result* of death, not death in itself. Physical death occurs when the body can no longer function, and when the human body dies, then the soul can no longer reside in it, so the separation occurs. Similarly, the separation of the human soul from God is the result of spiritual death and not the death itself. Spiritual death, the absence of God's *zoe* life, came to the human race by an act of disobedience, and as a result God removed his close fellowship from humanity. A spiritually dead person does not seek God and cannot understand or respond to God (1 Corinthians 2:14). Likewise, God cannot commune with the spiritually dead; there is no point in speaking to them since the dead cannot hear or talk back. It is only through the gift of God's *zoe* life that we can be awakened from death and reconciled back to God to enjoy fellowship with him.

In his sermon to the household of Cornelius, the Apostle Peter told his audience that God appointed Christ as the One who at the final judgment will judge "the living and the dead." (Acts 10:42) Paul made an identical statement to Timothy (2 Timothy 4:1). Based on all that we have reviewed in this book, the "dead" in these passages refers to the wicked who are dead in their sins, whose lives have been lived, and who have no further hope of redemption—while the "living" refers to those who are spiritually alive through faith. They are God's sheep, the redeemed.

Final death is referred to as the "second death" in Revelation 2, 20, and 21. What, then, is the first death? It is probably the death that resulted from Adam's sin that came to all humanity, encompassing both spiritual and physical death. Jesus said to the church in Smyrna in Revelation 2:11 that "he who overcomes will not be hurt at all by the second death," meaning the righteous will not be destroyed in the lake of fire. The wicked, on the other hand, are spiritually dead up to the point of physical death, and then spiritually dead up to the final judgment. But after the final judgment and punishment, they will experience the "second death," which is the complete and final death of both body and soul.

One fact frequently overlooked in relation to how God punishes sin is the reality of the death of Christ. It cannot be disputed that God sent Jesus to die for us on the cross to be punished for our sins. Not only was Christ's death the payment for our sins, but it was the quintessential example of how God punishes sin: by death. That he died in our place is demonstrated by the story of the release of Barabbas in place of Christ at his trial before Pilate. Barabbas the guilty was released into freedom, while Jesus the innocent was condemned and sent to die (Matthew 27:20-26). But Christ's punishment for our sins had a limited duration; it did not go on forever. If Jesus bore the punishment for our sins, then the penalty for sins cannot be an eternity of suffering and pain, since Jesus never experienced this. Christ's one death was the substitution for our death, which for each of us was to be exactly what Barabbas was sentenced to experience: an irreversible point-in-time execution, not an ongoing ordeal of torture.

There are those that contend that Christ's suffering and death was somehow experienced by him into eternity. Since the punishment for sin is eternal death as defined by Augustine, they reason, then Christ himself must have suffered an eternal death as well when he paid the price for our sins. Some, in fact, believe that Jesus somehow suffered millions of eternities in hell on the cross, all compacted into that one event in the total aggregated eternal torment that all mankind would have suffered had he not died for us. This amounts to speculative chain-link theology based solely on Augustine's premises of the immortality of the soul and eternal death.

It is true that Jesus was the perfect sacrifice and paid the price for the sin of all humanity past, present, and future—but that this process went on into eternity is pure conjecture and a great stretch of logic. By this reasoning, Christ must *still* be suffering his death continually now and forever. The clear teaching of Scripture is that it was the infinite value, purity, and perfect obedience of the One being sacrificed that paid for the sin of all humanity for all time, *not* the duration of time spent in anguish by the sin-bearer (see Hebrews chapters 4-10). Jesus did not suffer eternally because humans do not, either.

After his earthly suffering, Christ rose from the dead and is now seated in heaven with the Father. His perfect obedience to the Father and his subsequent suffering resulted in our eternal salvation. But his suffering was temporary so that afterward he would have victory over death. Jesus now lives forever, interceding for us as our high priest. His victory was also our victory, and we now share with Christ the glory and joy of salvation now and forever. As this fourth century Byzantine Liturgy of St. James so beautifully communicates:

Let all mortal flesh keep silence, And with fear and trembling stand;

Ponder nothing earthly minded, For with blessing in his hand

Christ our God to earth descendeth, Our full homage to demand.

King of kings, yet born of Mary, As of old on earth he stood,

Lord of lords in human vesture, In the Body and the Blood

He will give to all the faithful His own self for heavenly food.

TWO RESURRECTIONS

As introduced in Chapter 7, Job is thought of as one of the greatest biblical examples of patience and faith in the midst of suffering. In spite of all his troubles, Job knew that a day was coming when the righteous would live to stand before God's presence. Even in the midst of deep depression and anguish, he made this incredible statement: "I know that my Redeemer lives, and that in the end he will stand upon the earth. And after my skin has been destroyed, yet in my flesh I will see God; I myself will see him with my own eyes—I and not another. How my heart yearns within me." (Job 19:25-27)

Yet his understanding of that event, known to New Testament believers as the resurrection of the dead, was incomplete. Jesus himself provided great clarity to the resurrection in his concise description of the end times events in John 5:27-29. Speaking of the Father and himself, Christ said, "And he has given him authority to judge because he is the Son of Man. Do not be amazed at this, for a time is coming when all who are in their graves will hear his voice and come out—those who have done good will rise to live, and those who have done evil will rise to be condemned." This is a forceful declaration by Jesus himself of his authority to judge all people at the final judgment, and of the power of God to raise the dead to summon all people to that event.

Further detail is found in Revelation 20:1-10, which states in verse 4-5, "They came to life and reigned with Christ a thousand years … This is the first resurrection," referring to those who were martyred by the "beast" or had not worshiped him. Just as there are the first and second deaths in Revelation, likewise there are the first and second resurrections. Those who believe in a literal millennial reign of Christ interpret this passage to mean that the righteous will be raised in the first resurrection at the coming of Christ and then reign with Jesus for 1,000 years up until the final judgment.

Then Revelation 20:6 concludes, "Blessed and holy are those who have part in the first resurrection. The second death has no power over them." There is some disagreement whether all true believers who died before the second coming of Christ are included in this promise since the context refers to martyrs, but it seems it is so because we know that no true believers will experience the second death. Most evangelical Christians believe that the event described by Paul in I Thessalonians 4:16 is the first resurrection. It states, "For the Lord himself will come down from heaven, with a loud command, with the voice of the archangel and the trumpet call of God, and the dead in Christ will rise first. After that, we who are still alive and are left will be caught up together with them in the clouds to meet the lord in the air. And so we will be with the Lord forever."

The second resurrection is not mentioned specifically but is implied in the declaration of Revelation 20:12: "And I saw the dead, great and small, standing before the throne, and the books were opened." God will summon all people to the judgment. Most commentators believe that the majority of the righteous dead will have been raised already in the first resurrection, while the wicked who are not alive at the time will be raised for the express purpose of appearing before God. After the 1,000 year reign, the believers who have died during that time period will also be awakened at the second resurrection to appear before God for the final judgment, clothed in their new glorified bodies.

It is not even certain that the actual physical bodies the wicked inhabited while on earth will be resurrected for the judgment. This seems unlikely since these bodies will have already been decomposed, destroyed by the grave. Perhaps they will be given some bodily form to identify them while appearing before God. Whatever the case, their souls will be present and conscious and in some bodily form.

The prophet Daniel received a vision from God through which he was given a look at the end times. "At that time Michael, the great prince who protects your people, will arise. There will be a time of distress such has not happened from the beginning of nations until then. But at that time your people—everyone whose name is found written in the book—will be delivered. Multitudes who sleep in the dust of the earth will awake, some to everlasting life, others to shame and everlasting contempt. Those who are wise will shine like the brightness of the heavens, and those who lead many to righteousness, like the stars forever and ever." (Daniel 12:1-3)

The prophecy in Daniel's vision, similar to that of John 5:27-29, seems to condense all of the major events of the end times into one short summary. Some commentators believe that the descriptions of the resurrection provided in the Daniel 12 and John 5 passages are simplified and include both the first and second resurrections. However, this view does not easily accommodate the millennial reign of Christ of Revelation 20. Still, Daniel's description of the resurrection seems to parallel the second resurrection of Revelation 20 where the dead will be raised to appear before God at the final judgment. Those whose names were recorded in God's book of life will be delivered into everlasting life, while the wicked will suffer shame and contempt as their lives and deeds are displayed by God. The wise, or righteous, will shine the light of the Lord into eternity, forever displaying God's glory.

Chapter 16

All Things New

During the years that my family ministered in the remote mountain areas of Mexico, we lived with and got to know many of the indigenous people who lived in a small community miles away from civilization with no running water, electricity, or a hospital. At first, authentic Christian faith was scarce, with the church there consisting of a tiny group of about 10 believers. Living conditions were harsh and the people were well familiar with death. The average life expectancy was only about 50 years, and the infant mortality rate was somewhere between 30 and 50 percent. We witnessed the passing of a number of babies, mostly from the effects of water-borne and hygiene-related diseases and poor nutrition. Often, parents didn't even name their children until they were six months old. Only then did they feel confident their infants were going to survive.

One woman, Maria Corpus, visited our home regularly to drink coffee, visit, and trade goods with us for things she needed. She was a humble, soft-spoken woman who, along with her husband Ramos, were subsistence farmers, living off what could be grown on their small plot of land. Maria was especially drawn to my wife Nancy and her kind, welcoming spirit. During our first year there, Maria had two children but had previously lost one baby. She later became pregnant again and gave birth to a healthy baby girl. After six months, the baby was named Esperanza (Spanish for "hope")—and Maria brought the child with her when she visited us.

Sometime later, Maria came to our house one day distraught, broken, and alone. She told us Esperanza had died. She was only one year old. There was nothing that could be done, and now instead of paying a visit she was coming to ask us to take part in the burial of the child. Death was feared by most of the indigenous people, and burials were attended by only those that were required to be there, so the grief of loss was usually shared by just a few. Although she was not a follower of Christ, Maria's request showed that she trusted us and wanted us to share her and her husbands' pain—and perhaps provide some meaning to what had happened.

From our perspective, it didn't seem right that one so young who was made in God's image wasn't able to experience the joy, happiness, and love of her family and live out her life like the rest of us. For that matter, it didn't seem fair that many others in that community would also meet an early death. For most in that area, life was hard and sickness, despair, and grief were commonplace. Human sin, selfishness, and fear just compounded their effects and made life even more difficult. Our lives when in the United States had no such struggles. Our problems were insignificant in comparison. Each time we returned home the contrast was so stark it seemed like we had arrived in a completely foreign world. Sometimes, we felt guilty just for being there. We frequently asked ourselves, "Why were we born into a life of affluence and relative ease, but these people were born into a life of such trial and suffering?"

Questions and answers

We also saw how the truth of the gospel was readily available in America, but wasn't valued by many and often taken for granted—and we wondered why we were privileged to have known the way of truth from an early age, while the people we served in Mexico lived in what seemed to us as thick spiritual darkness? Our questions echoed Jeremiah's complaint before God: "Why do all the faithless live at ease? You have planted them, and they have taken root; they grow and bear fruit. You are always on their lips but far from their hearts." (Jeremiah 12:1-2) We also asked ourselves, "Why do some die early, and others live a full life, regardless of their spiritual condition?"

To answer these questions, we have to look deeper into Scripture and consider the promises God gave to us, as well as his plans for this world.

Most people realize that the world, in its present state, is not what it should be. Even optimists realize there are injustices in the world and many things wrong with the present state of humanity and the human experience. We all sense that God has created us for something better than difficulty, evil, despair, and finally death. We long for the time when everything will be put back right again. Those who are non-religious but still have a belief in a God can see the difference between what a good God would theoretically create and the actual conditions they see themselves living in, and they hope for a better world. Christians especially know that the world is presently not the way it was intended to be, and have the hope that God will someday make everything fit back into his plan. They understand that sickness and death, and human sin and rebellion against God's commands, characterize the fallen world and make it an extremely a difficult place to live in—and believe God has promised to reverse and correct what has gone wrong. Believers in Jesus wait for not only for their own redemption, but the redemption of all creation so that God's will and purpose will extend seamlessly throughout the whole universe.

Scripture gives us all hope. In 1 Corinthians 15, the Apostle Paul describes the progression of events at the end of human history and the consummation of God's eternal plan. "For as in Adam all die, so in Christ all will be made alive. But each in his own turn: Christ, the firstfruits; then, when he comes, those who belong to him." This refers to Christ's resurrection and the first resurrection of the dead. Paul continued, "Then the end will come, when he hands over the kingdom to God the Father after he has destroyed all dominion, authority and power. For he must reign until he has put all his enemies under his feet. The last enemy to be destroyed is death. For he 'has put everything under his feet' ... When he has done this, then the Son himself will be made subject to him who put everything under him, so that God may be all in all." (1 Corinthians 15:22-28) The promise is that Christ will raise to life those who belong to him, and then he will establish his kingdom until all of his enemies are subjected to him. Finally, he will destroy death and evil, and then give the kingdom over to God the Father who will then fill the universe.

Revelation 21 also describes the new order of creation after the final judgment is over. It speaks of a new heaven and new Earth where God's people will be eternally united with him in the dwelling he prepared for them. Of particular interest is the statement in Revelation 21:4-5 that "there will be no more death or mourning or crying or pain, for the old order of things has passed away ... I am making everything new!" In the world to come, there will be no more death because both death and the place of the dead will have been destroyed.

The writer of the book of Hebrews assures his readers of a kingdom that is permanent and unshakable. Speaking of God's voice during the Lord's encounter with Moses on Mount Sinai, he said, "At that time his voice shook the earth, but now he has promised, 'Once more I will shake not only the earth but also the heavens.' The words 'once more' indicate the removing of what can be shaken—that is, created things—so that what cannot be shaken may remain. Therefore, since we are receiving a kingdom that cannot be shaken, let us be thankful, and so worship God acceptably with reverence and awe, for our 'God is a consuming fire.'" (Hebrews 12:26-29) With his immense power, God will reorder our present world so that everything that is perishable will be destroyed, and what remains are his indestructible and eternal kingdom and all who inhabit it.

The fact that the wicked will not be preserved in the new order is confirmed in Revelation 21:8 describing the inhabitants of the new Jerusalem. "But the cowardly, the unbelieving, the vile, the murderers, the sexually immoral, those who practice magic arts, the idolaters and all liars—their place will be in the fiery lake of burning sulfur. This is the second death." This truth is reiterated in Revelation 22:14-15. "Blessed are those who wash their robes, that they may have the right to the tree of life and may go through the gates into the city. Outside are the dogs, those who practice magic arts, the sexually immoral, the murderers, the idolaters and everyone who loves and practices falsehood." Some commentators insist that the wording "outside are" shows that the wicked will still exist after the final judgment. However, the context of Revelation 22:7-21 is a final exhortation that provides warnings based on the messages from the entire book of Revelation. Verses 14-15 are not meant to accurately describe heaven and hell, but specifically to restate who have the right to enter the new heavenly city—and those who are excluded. Isaiah 52:1 presents a similar message: "Awake, awake, O Zion, clothe yourself with strength. Put on your garments of splendor, O Jerusalem, the holy city. The uncircumcised and defiled will not enter you again."

If there will be no death in this new order, then how can the spiritually dead "live" in hell and experience pain and anguish forever? Will God establish some faraway place or separate universe where the dead and the wicked still exist? How does such an idea correspond to Revelation 21 when God makes *all* things new, or 1 Corinthians 15 when God fills the universe, or Hebrews 12 when those things that can be shaken will be removed?

The only way it could happen is by God maintaining two separate realms—one for his new creation and the other for his old order which still contains sin, suffering, rebellion, and spiritual death. This describes Augustine's two kingdoms where heaven and hell go on in parallel existence forever, as well as the philosopher Mani's eternal coexistence of good and evil where neither ever wins. Such a second realm would however stain God's new creation and dilute the promise of God making "all things new" and being "all in all." It is not a good habit to take these great promises and make exceptions to conform to our theology. It is much better to take the promises of God at their face value and full meaning—that God will indeed make all things new, will exclude from the new order anything that does not serve his purpose, and will reorder the universe for an entirely new purpose. Clearly, in God's new order in eternity, the wicked will not be preserved in any form. The Lord is not obligated to keep alive in the world to come those who have no love for him.

The main themes of the book of Revelation are that God will be victorious over death and all evil, his kingdom will have no end, and that Christ will assume the Father's authority and rule forever. Death and fear of death, Satan's main weapons of control, will be destroyed. Satan will not rule an eternal kingdom; instead, his power will be completely obliterated. This is the very reason Satan is filled with fear and rage in the last days, because he knows his time is short (Revelation 12:12).

The vision of the last days found in Daniel 7 parallels these themes perfectly. In it, one "like a son of man" (a reference to Christ the Messiah) receives the Kingdom of God from "the Ancient of Days" (God the Father). In addition, four "great beasts" (representing four dominant kingdoms that rule the Earth) are described. The fourth kingdom is led by a boastful and oppressive king who wages war against the Lord and his saints. This will be the last earthly king to oppose God and his people, and is thought by many to be a personification of Satan himself, the Antichrist. He will fight in one last attempt to retain his authority on Earth, but this king and his kingdom will fail. "His power will be taken away and completely destroyed forever. Then the sovereignty, power and greatness of the kingdoms under the whole heaven will be handed over to the saints, the people of the Most High. His kingdom will be an everlasting kingdom, and all the rulers will worship and obey him." (Daniel 7:26-27)

Satan is not an opposite and equal power to God; he is a created being fully dependent on the Creator for his existence. God has no equal. He alone rules the universe. Satan's kingdom will be destroyed forever and replaced by the reign of the Most High, whose full authority and power are given to Jesus Christ. Any teaching or theology that ignores or contradicts these truths should be rejected.

In the present age, although God's presence fills the universe, his purposes are still not fulfilled since death, evil, sin, and rebellion exist. In the final age, God will not only be omnipresent, but he will destroy all that opposes his purposes. Everything and everyone that has rebelled against God and that does not serve his purpose, including death itself, will come to an absolute end. Then he will be "all in all," and the redeemed will enjoy his presence for eternity.

Isaiah 51:11 describes the joy of the redeemed as they will enter the heavenly city. "The ransomed of the Lord will return. They will enter Zion with singing; everlasting joy will crown their heads. Gladness and joy will overtake them, and sorrow and sighing will flee away." What a glorious day that will be when God's people enter their eternal home to dwell with him forever!

A divine reminder, an eternal hope

The burial for little Esperanza was simple. No one else came to help with the final preparations. There were no other relatives, friends, or neighbors. Ramos nailed together a basic casket from pine boards and placed into it the body of his daughter. Maria put a small cross on her little chest and folded her hands over it. They took a final look at their daughter and then nailed the lid shut. The procession was small, and it was indeed an obscure event, occurring in one small corner of the world and noticed by no one of importance.

But as we carried the casket from their small home, across their cornfield, and up the hill to the gravesite, I had a feeling that we were participating in something that was much greater than that humble setting suggested. We had been a part of burials before, but this occasion was a most unusual experience; in the midst of the sorrow, I felt a great sense of the glory of God—and that behind the scenes, in the midst of suffering and pain, his unshakable kingdom was expanding.

We arrived at the gravesite and were joined by several of the believing community members who did not fear death like the others. We read a few scriptures, talked briefly about Christ's death and his promise of eternal life, and prayed. Seeds of the gospel were planted. The small wooden casket was let down, Maria placed her daughter's clothes over it, and then it was covered over with soil. The grieving parents thanked us, then we all went back to our homes.

With time, the local church there began to grow and become established. We eventually moved to another location in Mexico and lost touch with Maria and Ramos. To this day, we do not know how they responded to the light of the gospel that was shown to them then, or later by others over the course of their lives. We do not know their eternal future or that of their children; only God knows. But through that experience, I was reminded by God that while the present life can bring sadness and despair, his promise of "all things new" was still valid, had not changed, and was going to be fulfilled someday.

Sometimes it seems there is much more evil in the world than goodness and holiness, much more suffering and sadness than rejoicing, much more despair than hope—and then comes the inevitable for all of us: death. It may be true that our present difficulties seem to outweigh everything else, but God's promise is that he will someday destroy them all, and they will all be gone. The only things that will remain will be eternal: the good, the holy, and the great joyous celebration of God's people with their Creator.

Those that we have been privileged to know and touch are only a small number amongst the billions of people that have lived on this Earth, each having been given light by God and an opportunity to respond to his love. His kingdom is expanding and growing, and is moving toward the end point. We know that God is a kind, loving, and just God, and he wants those he created in his image to enter into an eternal relationship with him, and will by no means turn away those who seek him.

God has called—and is now calling—whoever will to partake of his infinite goodness, holiness, and life, and to dwell with and rejoice with him forever in a glorious future which he is now preparing and will never end. This glory awaits those that respond to him and love him, and an indescribable reward awaits those that serve him.

"Behold, I will create new heavens and a new earth. The former things will not be remembered, nor will they come to mind. But be glad and rejoice forever in what I will create, for I will create Jerusalem to be a delight and its people a joy. I will rejoice over Jerusalem and take delight in my people; the sound of weeping and crying will be heard in it no more." (Isaiah 65:17-19)

Author's End Note

Hopefully, *Final Judgment & the Goodness of God* will cause you to conduct a more in-depth study of the relevant Bible passages cited in this book and search the scriptures, as the Bereans did, to see if these things are true. In doing so, you may question the conventional beliefs about final judgment and open to other views that more conform to the character of God as presented in the Bible. If that happens, God will surely have blessed you in your search.

There have been other writers who have treated each of the topics covered in this book more thoroughly and convincingly, and in much more detail. For a deeper understanding of final judgment and punishment in the Bible, the works of the following authors are recommended. In my opinion, those authors that defend the traditional views of hell and judgment seem to rely more on logic and extrapolation than Scripture. The authors listed below, in addition to being respected and accomplished scholars and theologians, have researched these topics thoroughly and have come to their conclusions by sound biblical exegesis.

Atkinson, B. F. C., *Life and Immortality*, in: Rethinking Hell, Readings in Evangelical Conditionalism, edited by C. M. Date, G.G. Stump, and J. W. Anderson, 2014

Fudge, E.W., *The Fire That Consumes*, Verdict Publications, 1982

Hughes, P. E., *The True Image*, Wm. B. Eerdmans Publishing Company, 1989

Marshall, C. D., *Beyond Retribution*, Wm. B. Eerdmans Publishing Company, 2001

Stott, John R.W., *Judgment and Hell* in: Evangelical Essentials: A Liberal-Evangelical Dialogue, Questions from David Edwards, Intervarsity Press, 1989.

Wenham, J. *The Case for Conditional Immortality*, Fourth Edinburgh Conference on Christian Dogmatics, 1991.

A good collection of short works and excerpts by various authors (including those listed above) is:

Rethinking Hell, Readings in Evangelical Conditionalism, Edited by C. M. Date, G.G. Stump, and J. W. Anderson, Cascade Books, Wipf and Stock Publishers, 2014.

Made in the USA
San Bernardino, CA
30 March 2019